THE CALIFORNIA DIRECTORY OF
FINE WINERIES

Brian D. Sullivan
Local

FOURTH EDITION

THE CALIFORNIA DIRECTORY OF
FineWineries

MARTY OLMSTEAD, WRITER

ROBERT HOLMES, PHOTOGRAPHER

TOM SILBERKLEIT, EDITOR AND PUBLISHER

WINE HOUSE PRESS

Contents

INTRODUCTION

Whether you are a visitor or a native seeking the ultimate chalice of nectar from the grape, navigating Northern California's wine country can be intimidating. Hundreds of wineries—from glamorous estates to converted barns, from nationally recognized labels to hidden gems—are found throughout Napa, Sonoma, and Mendocino. The challenge is deciding where to go and how to plan a trip. This book will be your indispensable traveling companion.

The sixty-nine wineries in this fully updated, fourth edition of *The California Directory of Fine Wineries* are known for producing some of the world's most admired wines. From the moment you walk in the door of these wineries, you will be greeted like a guest and invited to sample at a relaxing, leisurely tempo. Although the quality of the winemaker's art is of paramount importance, the wineries are also notable as tourist destinations. Many boast award-winning contemporary architecture, while others are housed in lovingly preserved historical structures. Some have galleries featuring museum-quality artwork by local and international artists or exhibits focusing on the region's past and the history of winemaking. You will also enjoy taking informative behind-the-scenes tours, exploring inspirational gardens, and participating in celebrated culinary programs. With a bit of advance planning, you can arrange to take part in a barrel sampling, a blending seminar, or a grape stomping.

As you explore this magnificent region, you'll encounter some of California's most appealing scenery and attractions—mountain ranges, rugged coastline, pastures with majestic oak trees, abundant parkland, renowned spas, and historic towns. Use the information in this book to plan your trip, and be sure to stop along the way and take in the sights. You have my promise that traveling to your destination will be as pleasurable as the wine tasted upon your welcome.

—Tom Silberkleit
Editor and Publisher
Wine House Press
Sonoma, California

THE ETIQUETTE OF WINE TASTING

Most of the wineries profiled in this book offer amenities ranging from lush gardens to art exhibitions, but their main attraction is the tasting room. This is where winery employees get a chance to share their products and knowledge with consumers, in hopes of establishing a lifelong relationship. They are there to please.

Yet, for some visitors, the ritual of tasting fine wines can be intimidating. Perhaps it's because swirling wine and using a spit bucket seem to be unnatural acts. But with a few tips, even a first-time taster can enjoy the experience. After all, the point of tasting is to enhance your knowledge by learning the differences among varieties of wines, styles of winemaking, and appellations.

A list of available wines is usually posted, beginning with whites and ending with the heaviest reds or, if available, dessert wines. Look for the tasting notes, which are typically set out on the counter; refer to them as you taste each wine. A number of wineries charge a tasting fee for three or four wines of your choosing or for a "flight"—most often three preselected wines. In any event, the tasting process is the same.

After you are served, hold the stem of the glass with your thumb and as many fingers as you need to maintain control. Lift the glass up to the light and note the color and intensity of the wine. Good wines tend to be bright, with the color fading near the rim. Next, gently swirl the wine in the glass. Observe how much of the wine adheres to the sides of the glass. If lines—called legs—are visible, the wine is viscous, indicating body or weight as well as a high alcohol content. Now, tip the glass to about a 45-degree angle, take a short sniff, and concentrate on the aromas. Swirl the wine again to aerate it, releasing additional aromas. Take another sniff and see if the "bouquet" reminds you of anything—rose petals, citrus fruit, or a freshly ironed pillowcase, for example—that will help you identify the aroma.

Finally, take a sip and swirl the wine around your tongue, letting your taste buds pick up all the flavors. The wine may remind you of honey or cherries or mint—as with the "nosing," try to make as many associations as you can. Then spit the wine into the bucket on the counter. Afterward, notice how long the flavor stays in your mouth; a long finish is the ideal. If you don't want another taste, just pour the wine remaining in your glass into the bucket and move on. Remember, the more you spit or pour out, the more wines you can sample.

The next level of wine tasting involves guided tastings and food-and-wine pairings. In these sessions, a few cheeses or a series of appetizers are paired with a flight of wines, usually a selection of three red or three white wines presented in the recommended order of tasting. The server will explain what goes with what.

If you still feel self-conscious, practice at home. Once you are in a real tasting room, you'll be better able to focus on the wine itself. That's the real payoff, because once you learn what you like and why you like it, you'll be able to recognize wines in a similar vein anywhere in the world.

What Is an Appellation?

The word *appellation* is often used to refer to the geographical area where wine grapes were grown. If the appellation is named on the bottle label, it means that at least 85 percent of the wine is from that area.

The terms "appellation of origin" and "American Viticultural Area" (AVA) are frequently used interchangeably in casual conversation, but they are not synonymous. In the United States, appellations follow geopolitical borders, such as state and county lines, rather than geographic boundaries. AVAs are defined by such natural features as soil types, climate, and topography.

Since 1978 the U.S. Bureau of Alcohol, Tobacco and Firearms (BATF) has been the arbiter of what does and does not qualify as an AVA. A winery or other interested party that wants a particular area to qualify as an official AVA must supply proof to the BATF that it has enough specific attributes to distinguish it significantly from its neighbors.

Why do winemakers care? Because it is far more prestigious—and informative—to label a wine with an appellation such as Sonoma County, Napa Valley, or Russian River Valley than with the more generic California, which means the grapes could have come from the Central Valley or anywhere else in the state. Moreover, informed consumers learn that a Chardonnay from the Alexander Valley, for instance, is apt to smell and taste different from one originating in the Russian River Valley. A winery may be located in one appellation but use grapes from another to make a particular wine. In this case, the appellation on the label would indicate the source of the grapes rather than the physical location of the winery.

The following are the appellations in Napa, Sonoma, and Mendocino:

Napa	Sonoma	Mendocino
Atlas Peak	Alexander Valley	Anderson Valley
Chiles Valley District	Bennett Valley	Cole Ranch
Diamond Mountain District	Chalk Hill	Dos Rios
Howell Mountain	Dry Creek Valley	McDowell Valley
Los Carneros	Green Valley	Mendocino
Mount Veeder	Knight's Valley	Mendocino Ridge
Napa Valley	Los Carneros	North Coast
North Coast	North Coast	Potter Valley
Oak Knoll District	Northern Sonoma	Redwood Valley
Oakville	Rockpile	Sanel Valley
Rutherford	Russian River Valley	(proposed viticultural area)
Spring Mountain District	Sonoma Coast	Ukiah Valley
St. Helena	Sonoma Mountain	(proposed viticultural area)
Stags Leap District	Sonoma Valley	Yorkville Highlands
Wild Horse Valley		
Yountville		

NAPA

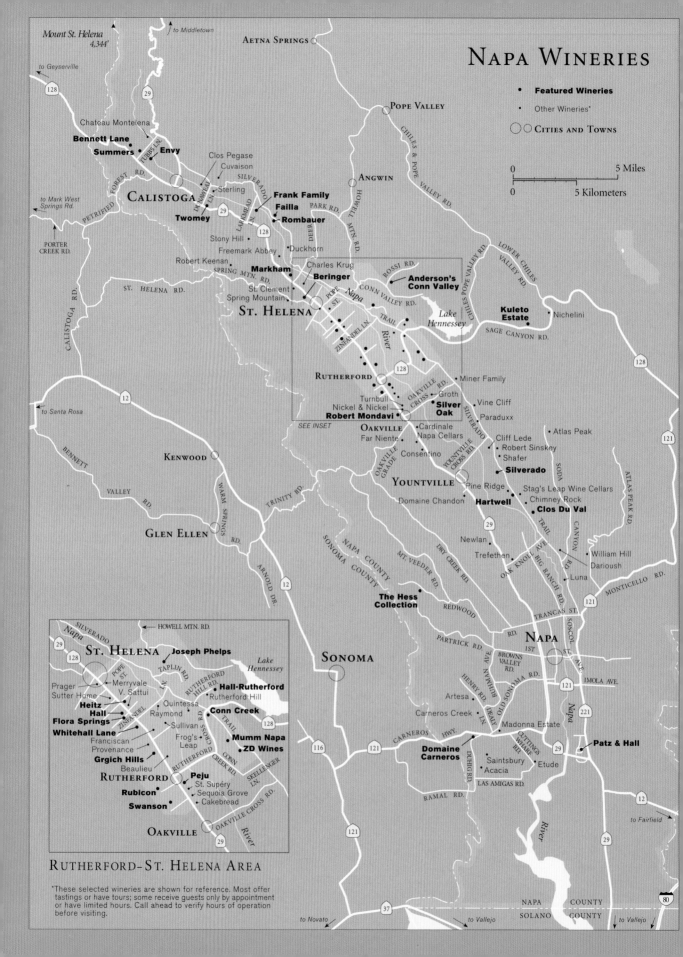

NAPA WINERIES

Mount St. Helena
4,344'

to Middletown →

AETNA SPRINGS

to Geyserville →

128

29

Chateau Montelena

Bennett Lane
Summers **Envy**

POPE VALLEY

ANGWIN

- Featured Wineries
- Other Wineries*
○○ CITIES AND TOWNS

0   5 Miles
0   5 Kilometers

Clos Pegase
Cuvaison
Sterling
SILVERADO

CALISTOGA

Frank Family
Failla
Twomey   **Rombauer**

128

Stony Hill
Freemark Abbey   • Duckhorn

Robert Keenan
SPRING MTN. RD.

Markham
Beringer

Anderson's Conn Valley

St. Clement
Spring Mountain

ST. HELENA

Kuleto Estate   • Nichelini

Lake Hennessey

SAGE CANYON RD.

128

RUTHERFORD

128

• Miner Family

Turnbull   Groth
Nickel & Nickel   **Silver Oak**
Robert Mondavi

Vine Cliff
Paraduxx

SEE INSET

• Cardinale
OAKVILLE   Napa Cellars
Far Niente   • Consentino

Cliff Lede
• Robert Sinskey
• Shafer

• Atlas Peak

Silverado

KENWOOD

YOUNTVILLE

Pine Ridge
Domaine Chandon   **Hartwell**

Stag's Leap Wine Cellars
Chimney Rock
Clos Du Val

GLEN ELLEN

to Santa Rosa →

12

Newlan
Trefethen

• William Hill
Darioush
• Luna

NAPA COUNTY
SONOMA COUNTY

The Hess Collection

REDWOOD

121

121

SONOMA

TRANCAS ST.

NAPA

221

RUTHERFORD–ST. HELENA AREA

← HOWELL MTN. RD.

SILVERADO
Napa

29
128

ST. HELENA   **Joseph Phelps**

Lake Hennessey

Prager   • Merryvale
Sutter Home   V. Sattui
Heitz   Quintessa
Hall   Raymond
Flora Springs   Sullivan
Whitehall Lane   Franciscan
Provenance
Grgich Hills   Beaulieu

RUTHERFORD   **Peju**
St. Supéry
Rubicon   Sequoia Grove
• Cakebread
Swanson

Hall-Rutherford
Rutherford Hill
Conn Creek

Mumm Napa
ZD Wines

128

OAKVILLE

29

Domaine Carneros

Artesa
Carneros Creek
Madonna Estate

Saintsbury
Acacia   • Etude

Patz & Hall

CARNEROS HWY.

LAS AMIGAS RD.
RAMAL RD.

116   121

37

to Novato →

to Vallejo →

NAPA   COUNTY
SOLANO   COUNTY

to Fairfield →

12

to Vallejo →

80

*These selected wineries are shown for reference. Most offer tastings or have tours; some receive guests only by appointment or have limited hours. Call ahead to verify hours of operation before visiting.

The most famous winemaking region in the United States, the Napa Valley is packed with hundreds of premium wineries and thousands of acres of vineyards amassed in a narrow valley less than thirty miles long. This patchwork of agriculture extends north from upper San Pablo Bay to the dramatic palisades towering above Calistoga. The valley is defined on the east by a series of hills known as the Vaca Range and on the west by the rugged peaks of the Mayacamas  Range, including the steep forested slopes of Mount Veeder.

St. Helena, where upscale shops line the historic Main Street, is the jewel in the region's crown. At the southern end of the valley, the city of Napa has experienced a boom in recent years, with a plethora of restaurants and attractions such as COPIA: The American Center for Wine, Food and the Arts and the vibrant Oxbow Public Market that opened in 2008. The mostly two-lane Highway 29 links these and smaller towns that welcome visitors with a variety of spas, restaurants, and boutique inns.

For an unforgettable impression, book a sunrise hot-air balloon ride or simply drive up the Oakville Grade and pull over at the top for a postcard-perfect view.

ANDERSON'S CONN VALLEY VINEYARDS

Less than a ten-minute drive from bustling downtown St. Helena, Anderson's Conn Valley Vineyards occupies a niche in a valley within a valley. The location is so remote that most drivers along Conn Valley Road aren't even aware the winery exists. Out here, you could hear a pin drop, except during the busy harvest season that begins in late summer.

Anderson's Conn Valley Vineyards was founded in 1983 by Gus and Todd Anderson along with their wives, Phyllis and Dana. Gus search for vineyard property in of realizing Napa's tremendous widely known (in the wake of the Napa on the world wine map) and prohibitively expensive.

Joseph Heitz and Joseph wineries in the neighborhood by dream site, forty acres in the eastern Anderson spearheaded the lengthy Napa Valley. He had the advantage potential before the region became famous 1976 Paris Tasting that put before land in wine country became

Phelps had already established the time the Andersons found their part of the St. Helena American Viticultural Area near the base of Howell Mountain. Unfortunately, the acreage was not for sale; it would take fifteen months of negotiations to secure the property.

Then the real work of establishing a winery operation began, and for the most part, it has all been done by the Andersons. Todd Anderson left his profession as a geophysicist to pound posts, hammer nails, and install twenty-six and a half acres of prime vineyards. That was just the beginning. While the vines matured, the Andersons created a fifteen-acre-foot reservoir and built the winery, the residence, and a modest cave system.

The family did hire professionals with the necessary heavy-duty equipment to expand the caves by eight thousand square feet. Completed in 2001, the nine-thousand-square-foot cave features a warren of narrow pathways beneath the hillside. Deep in the cavern, one wall has been pushed out to make way for tables and chairs where visitors can sample the wines. In clement weather, tastings are often held on the far side of the caves, with seating beneath market umbrellas at tables that overlook the reservoir.

Tours and tastings are led by Todd Anderson or his wife, Ronene, who now operate Anderson's Conn Valley Vineyards. A great advantage to touring a family winery is the chance to get to know the people behind the wines and to linger long enough to ask questions that might never get answered during a large group tour at one of Napa's big and better-known wineries located along Highway 29 or the Silverado Trail.

ANDERSON'S CONN VALLEY VINEYARDS
680 Rossi Rd.
St. Helena, CA 94574
707-963-8600
800-946-3497
info@connvalleyvineyards.com
www.connvalleyvineyards.com

OWNERS: Anderson family.

LOCATION: 3.3 miles east of Silverado Trail via Howell Mountain Rd. and Conn Valley Rd.

APPELLATION: Napa Valley.

HOURS: 10 A.M.–5 P.M. daily.

TASTINGS: By appointment. Complimentary for current release wines.

TOURS: By appointment.

THE WINES: Cabernet Sauvignon, Chardonnay, Pinot Noir, Sauvignon Blanc.

SPECIALTIES: Cabernet Sauvignon, Bordeaux blends.

WINEMAKER: Mac Sawyer.

ANNUAL PRODUCTION: 5,000 cases.

OF SPECIAL NOTE: Barrel tasting, lunch, and other special events are available at varying prices by advance arrangement. Tours and tastings are held in extensive winery caves.

NEARBY ATTRACTIONS: Bothe-Napa State Park (hiking, picnicking, horseback riding, swimming Memorial Day–Labor Day); Bale Grist Mill State Historic Park (water-powered mill circa 1846); Silverado Museum (Robert Louis Stevenson memorabilia).

BENNETT LANE WINERY

BENNETT LANE WINERY
3340 Hwy. 128
Calistoga, CA 94515
877-629-6272
info@bennettlane.com
www.bennettlane.com

OWNERS: Randy and Lisa Lynch.

LOCATION: About 2 miles north of Calistoga.

APPELLATION: Napa Valley.

HOURS: 10 A.M.–5:30 P.M. daily.

TASTINGS: $10 for 3 wines.

TOURS: Daily, by appointment.

THE WINES: Cabernet Sauvignon, Chardonnay, Maximus (a red blend), Port, White Maximus (a white blend).

SPECIALTIES: Cabernet Sauvignon, Maximus.

WINEMAKER: Rob Hunter.

ANNUAL PRODUCTION: 12,000 cases.

OF SPECIAL NOTE: Blending experiences for groups of 6 or more ($175 per person). Chocolate and Maximus tastings on Saturdays (complimentary with tasting fee). Reserve Chardonnay and Port available only at tasting room. Annual events include Cabernet Release Weekend (February).

NEARBY ATTRACTIONS: Old Faithful Geyser of California; Robert Louis Stevenson State Park (hiking).

Far from the din and traffic of central Napa Valley, Bennett Lane Winery lures the adventure-some Cabernet lover to the northernmost wedge of the valley, where the Vaca Range meets the Mayacamas Range. This sequestered setting just north of the town of Calistoga features dramatic views of Mount St. Helena and the Palisades as well as a manicured lawn for picnicking in peace. It is an ideal backdrop for Bennett Lane's hand-crafted, small-production wines.

At the front end of the Mediterranean-style winery, a small, sparsely decorated tasting room fits the low-key ambience of the surroundings. Nothing inside or out would suggest that

the winery belongs to a pair of dyed-in-the-wool NASCAR aficionados. For owners Lisa and Randy Lynch, there is no conflict of interest. Race cars and racy reds share a certain sex appeal. Their love of wine happened to mesh with another major interest. At a time when few would have considered promoting fine wines and fast cars in the same breath, Randy has created a winning strategy. He and Lisa were the first California vintners to own a NASCAR team, which proudly sports the winery's logo as it tours the western United States. (Although the team races in the western circuit, one of its NASCAR Fords can often be seen at the winery.)

The Lynches were relative newcomers to the world of wine in 2003 when they purchased what had been a custom crush facility. Soon after, they brought on Rob Hunter as winemaker. Hunter, a twenty-five-year wine industry veteran and the former vice president and director of winemaking for Sterling Vineyards, works closely with Bennett Lane's vineyard manager, Doug Wight. Both are considered among the best in the business. Today, the Lynches own ten acres on the winery property, as well as twelve acres surrounding their house on Tubbs Lane in Calistoga. They also source fruit from more than forty acres of vineyards in the Napa Valley.

Bennett Lane's signature wine is named Maximus, after the second-century Roman emperor Magnus Maximus, a noted vinophile of his day. The exact percentages of varietals that go into the Maximus wines vary somewhat from vintage to vintage. The 2005 Maximus Red Feasting Wine is a typical blend, with 64 percent Cabernet Sauvignon, 25 percent Merlot, and 11 percent Syrah. At Bennett Lane, blending is the name of the game—and visitors can play, too. The winery offers groups of six or more a custom experience that includes a blending session led by Bennett Lane's expert staff, a souvenir bottle of individually blended wine for each guest, and a private wine-and-cheese pairing.

BERINGER VINEYARDS

With the 1883 Rhine House, hand-carved aging tunnels, and a heritage dating to 1876, Beringer Vineyards is steeped in history like few other wineries in California. The oldest continuously operating winery in the Napa Valley, it combines age-old traditions with up-to-date technology to create a wide range of award-winning wines.

It was German know-how that set the Beringer brothers on the path to glory. Jacob and Frederick Beringer emigrated from Mainz, Germany, to the United States in the 1860s. Jacob, having worked in cellars in Germany, was intrigued when he heard that the California climate was ideal for growing the  varietal grapes that flourished in Europe's winemaking regions. Leaving Frederick in New York, he traveled west in 1870 to discover that the Napa Valley's rocky, well-drained soils were similar to those in his native Rhine Valley. Five years later, he bought land with Frederick and began excavating the hillsides to create tunnels for aging his wines. The brothers founded Beringer Vineyards in 1876. During the building of the caves and winery, Jacob lived in an 1848 farmhouse now known as the Hudson House. The meticulously restored and expanded structure now serves as Beringer Vineyards' Culinary Arts Center.

But the star attraction on the lavishly landscaped grounds is unquestionably the seventeen-room Rhine House, which Frederick modeled after his ancestral home in Germany. The redwood, brick, and stucco mansion is painted in the original Tudor color scheme of earth tones, and the original slate still covers the gabled roof and exterior. The interior is graced with myriad gems of craftsmanship such as Belgian art nouveau–style stained-glass windows.

The winery's standard tour encompasses a visit to the cellars and the hand-dug aging tunnels in the Old Stone Winery, where tasting is available. Beringer also offers programs that provide visitors more in-depth experiences. The Vintage Legacy Tour, focusing on the winery's history, takes guests to the original St. Helena Home Vineyard, then to the Old Stone Winery for a barrel tasting, and finally to the Cellar Tasting Room to sample additional wines. The Historic District Tour emphasizes points of historic interest such as the Rhine House and the aging caves. The Taste of Beringer Tour covers the growing cycle of a grapevine and proceeds through the Old Stone Winery prior to a special wine tasting in the historic Rhine House.

BERINGER VINEYARDS
2000 Main St.
St. Helena, CA 94574
707-963-4812
www.beringer.com

LOCATION: On Hwy. 29 about .5 mile north of St. Helena.

APPELLATION: Napa Valley.

HOURS: 10 A.M.–5 P.M. daily in winter; until 6 P.M. in summer.

TASTINGS: 2 wines with tour fee; $5 for 3 nonreserve wines in Old Stone Winery; $5–16 for reserve wine flights.

TOURS: 30-minute tours ($10) on the hour, 10 A.M.– 4 P.M. Vintage Legacy Tour ($35), Historic District Tour ($20), and Taste of Beringer Tour ($15) by reservation.

THE WINES: Cabernet Franc, Cabernet Sauvignon, Cabernet Sauvignon Port, Chardonnay, Merlot, Pinot Noir, Sangiovese, Sauvignon Blanc, Syrah, White Merlot, White Zinfandel.

SPECIALTIES: Private Reserve Cabernet Sauvignon, single-vineyard Cabernet Sauvignon, Private Reserve Chardonnay.

WINEMAKERS: Ed Sbragia, wine master emeritus; Laurie Hook, winemaker.

ANNUAL PRODUCTION: Unavailable.

OF SPECIAL NOTE: Tour includes visit to barrel storage caves hand-chiseled by Chinese laborers in late 1800s.

NEARBY ATTRACTIONS: Bothe-Napa State Park (hiking, picnicking, horseback riding, swimming Memorial Day–Labor Day); Silverado Museum (Robert Louis Stevenson memorabilia).

CLOS DU VAL

CLOS DU VAL
5330 Silverado Trail
Napa, CA 94558
707-261-5200
800-993-9463
cdv@closduval.com
www.closduval.com

OWNER: John Goelet.

LOCATION: 5 miles north of the town of Napa.

APPELLATION: Napa Valley.

HOURS: 10 A.M.–5 P.M. daily.

TASTINGS: $10 for 4 wines (applicable to wine purchase); $20 for reserve wines (includes souvenir logo glass).

TOURS: By appointment.

THE WINES: Cabernet Sauvignon, Chardonnay, Merlot, Pinot Noir.

SPECIALTY: Cabernet Sauvignon.

WINEMAKER: John Clews.

ANNUAL PRODUCTION: 65,000 cases.

OF SPECIAL NOTE: *Pétanque* court and picnic areas. Reserve wines available only in the tasting room.

NEARBY ATTRACTIONS: COPIA: The American Center for Wine, Food and the Arts; Napa Valley Museum (winemaking displays, art exhibits); Napa Valley Opera House (live performances in historic building).

That this winery has a French name is not an affectation. Owner and cofounder John Goelet's mother was a direct descendant of Françoise Guestier, a native of Bordeaux who worked for the Marquis de Segur, owner of Chateau Lafite and Latour. Clos Du Val translates as "small vineyard estate of a small valley," a modest nomenclature for a winery of its stature.

When Goelet, who is also the son of an American entrepreneur, set out on a global search for premium vineyard land, he found the ideal partner in Bernard Portet. Born in Cognac and raised in Bordeaux, Portet is a descendant of six generations of winemakers. He followed his passion with formal studies at the French winemaking schools of Toulouse and Montpelier before Goelet hired him in 1970 to establish Clos Du Val.

Portet spent two years searching six continents before getting a taste of the Napa Valley climate—or, technically, its microclimates. At the time, the cool evenings and dramatic terrain of the Stags Leap District were relatively undiscovered by winemakers. Goelet proved his faith in Portet by promptly acquiring 150 acres of land in the district. The first vintage of the new venture was a 1972 Cabernet Sauvignon, one of only six California Cabernets selected for the now-legendary "Paris Tasting" in 1976, an event that put the world on notice that the Napa Valley was a winemaking force to watch. Ten years later, the same vintage took first place in a rematch, further enhancing Clos Du Val's reputation for creating wines that stand the test of time.

In 1973 Clos Du Val purchased 180 acres in another little-recognized appellation—Carneros in southern Napa. Thirteen years later, the winery released its first Carneros Chardonnay, and four years later, its first Carneros Pinot Noir.

A driveway lined with cypress trees leads to the imposing, vine-covered stone winery, behind which the dramatic rock outcroppings of Stags Leap rise in sharp relief. In front of the tasting room are Mediterranean-style gardens, a raised lawn area with tables and chairs defined by a hedge of boxwood, and a demonstration vineyard with twenty rows of Merlot grapevines, accompanied by brief explanations of vineyard management techniques. Inside the winery, halogen lights on the high ceiling beam down on the wooden tasting bar, the unglazed earth-toned tile floor, and a corner display of merchandise bearing the winery's distinctive, curlicued logo. Glass doors on the far side look into a large fermentation room filled with oak and steel tanks. Visitors are welcome to prolong their visit by playing *pétanque* or enjoying a picnic in the olive grove.

CONN CREEK WINERY

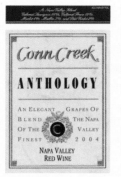

onn Creek is one of the easiest-to-find wineries in the Napa Valley. Located near a well-traveled Rutherford intersection, it is housed in a simple Spanish Mediterranean-style stucco building that blends in well with the surroundings. In front, a grove of olive trees and colorful perennials thrive year-round in the California sun.

The winery was founded by William Collins, a former submarine officer, and his wife, Kathy, who named it for a seasonal tributary of the Napa River that flows through their vineyards. They planted grapes in 1967 and, six years later, established the winery and produced their first vintage. Conn Creek quickly won recognition for its red wines, particularly the 1974 Eisele Vineyard Cabernet Sauvignon. Most of the grapes for the award-winning wines produced in the early years came from the Collins Vineyard, which is so rocky that the owners had to use dynamite to break up the soil before planting. Situated alongside Highway 29 in St. Helena, Collins Vineyard has fifty-four acres of Cabernet Sauvignon, Cabernet Franc, and Merlot. Although Collins sold his winery in 1986, he maintains an exclusive long-term grape contract with Conn Creek.

The new owners, Ste. Michelle Wine Estates, decided to devote their energies to producing world-class Cabernet-based red wines, paring Chardonnay and Zinfandel from the winery's product line to do so. The legendary André Tchelistcheff, the former winemaker at Beaulieu Vineyard and a longtime consultant to Ste. Michelle, participated in the winery's transition to limited-production Bordeaux varietals. By 1990 the winery had been retooled for its new focus, with an expanded barrel room, improved storage, and the acquisition of new French oak barrels. These changes were followed a year later with the release of Anthology, the winery's Bordeaux-style blend. More changes came in 2003, when the St. Helena winery was refurbished with enhancements to the winemaking facility, retail shop, and barrel blending room. It also had a new winemaker, Jeff McBride, who had been winemaker at both Kenwood Vineyards and Dry Creek Vineyard in Sonoma County.

Conn Creek Winery continues to pursue the goal of remaining a limited-production facility specializing in Napa Valley Cabernet Sauvignon. To meet the demand for its wines, the winery currently sources grapes from thirteen of the Napa Valley's subappellations, including its own estate vineyard in Rutherford; Collins Vineyard north of St. Helena ; Stagecoach Vineyard in Napa's rugged eastern hills, a prized growing area for Cabernet Franc and Merlot; and the Carneros in the cool southern part of Napa Valley.

CONN CREEK WINERY
8711 Silverado Trail
St. Helena, CA 94574
707-963-9100
info@conncreek.com
www.conncreek.com

OWNER: Ste. Michelle Wine Estates.

LOCATION: Intersection of Silverado Trail and Rutherford Cross Rd.

APPELLATION: Napa Valley.

HOURS: 11 A.M.–4 P.M. Sunday–Friday; 10 A.M.–4 P.M. Saturday.

TASTINGS: $10 for 6 wines; $25 for single-vineyard Cabernet Sauvignon flight.

TOURS: By appointment, 11 A.M.–3 P.M.

THE WINES: Anthology (red Bordeaux-style blend), Cabernet Franc, Cabernet Sauvignon, Sauvignon Blanc.

SPECIALTIES: Bordeaux varietals, especially Cabernet Sauvignon.

WINEMAKER: Jeff McBride.

ANNUAL PRODUCTION: 18,000 cases.

OF SPECIAL NOTE: Barrel sampling and blending seminars by appointment. Conn Creek Cabernet Franc, single-AVA Cabernet Sauvignons, and Sauvignon Blanc available only at tasting room, which also pours Villa Mt. Eden Grand Reserve Chardonnay, Pinot Noir, and vineyard-designated Zinfandels.

NEARBY ATTRACTIONS: Culinary Institute of America at Greystone (cooking demonstrations); Silverado Museum (Robert Louis Stevenson memorabilia).

DOMAINE CARNEROS

DOMAINE CARNEROS
1240 Duhig Rd.
Napa, CA 94559
800-716-BRUT (2788)
707-257-0101
www.domainecarneros.
com

OWNERS: Partnership
between Taittinger and
Kopf families.

LOCATION: Intersection of
Hwys. 121/12 and Duhig
Rd., 4 miles southwest
of the town of Napa and
6 miles southeast of
Sonoma.

APPELLATION: Los Carneros.

HOURS: 10 A.M.–6 P.M. daily.

TASTINGS: $7–$15 per glass,
depending on variety;
$15 for sampler of
3 sparkling wines or
$15 for 3 Pinot Noirs.

TOURS: 11 A.M., 1 P.M.,
and 3 P.M. daily. Group
tours for 10 or more by
appointment. Additional
tours available seasonally.

THE WINES: Brut Rosé,
Le Rêve, Pinot Noir,
Vintage Brut.

SPECIALTIES: *Méthode
champenoise* sparkling
wine, Pinot Noir.

WINEMAKER: Eileen Crane.

ANNUAL PRODUCTION:
48,000 cases.

OF SPECIAL NOTE: Table
service in salon or on
terrace with panoramic
views of Carneros region.
Cheese and caviar available
for purchase.

NEARBY ATTRACTIONS:
di Rosa Preserve (indoor
and outdoor exhibits of
works by contemporary Bay
Area artists); Napa Valley
Opera House.

An architectural tribute to its French heritage, the chateau that houses Domaine Carneros would look at home in Champagne, France. It dominates a hillside in the renowned Carneros region in southern Napa, prime growing area for the grape varieties that go into the best sparkling wine and sumptuous Pinot Noir. The opulent winery is approached by a long series of steps that climb to a grand entranceway. French marble floors, high ceilings, and decorative features such as a Louis XV fireplace mantel imbue the interior with a palatial ambience. Guests are welcome to order wines in the elegant salon, warmed by a fireplace on cool days, or on the terrace.

Established in 1987, Domaine Carneros is a joint venture between Cham- pagne Taittinger of France and Kobrand Corporation. President Director-General Claude Taittinger led the extensive search for the ideal site for making world-class sparkling wine. The Carneros region's long, moderately cool growing season and the fog that mitigates the summer heat allow for slow, even ripening and perfect acidic balance in the Pinot Noir and Chardonnay grapes. Domaine Carneros farms four vineyards totaling 350 hundred acres in the appellation.

Harvest at Domaine Carneros begins in mid-August, when workers head out to pick grapes before dawn. A delicate balance of sugar and acidity is required for the best sparkling wine. The fruit is immediately brought to the press for the gentle extracting of the juice. From that moment through vinification, each lot is maintained separately before the exact blend is determined. The sparkling wines are made in accordance with the traditional *méthode champenoise,* in which secondary fermentation takes place in the bottle, not the tank. The grapes for Pinot Noir are gathered several weeks after the sparkling wine harvest is complete, then are fermented for ten days. After this, the juices are siphoned off, and the fruit is gently pressed to extract the remaining juice. The resulting wine is aged in French oak barrels for up to ten months before bottling.

In charge of these elaborate procedures is president Eileen Crane, who began her career at Domaine Chandon and later served as winemaker and vice president of Gloria Ferrer Champagne Caves in nearby Sonoma. This experience made her the ideal choice for overseeing the planning and development of Domaine Carneros. Crane focuses on making the most of the winery's combination of exceptional vineyards and meticulous winemaking. Early in 2008, she achieved another milestone: Domaine Carneros became the first sparkling winery in the United States to have 100 percent of its estate vineyards certified as organic.

ENVY WINES

ENVY WINES
1170 Tubbs Ln.
Calistoga, CA 94515
707-942-4670
info@envywines.com
www.envywines.com

OWNERS: Mark Carter
and Nils Venge.

LOCATION: About 4 miles
north of Calistoga
via Hwy. 128 or the
Silverado Trail.

APPELLATION: Napa Valley.

HOURS: 10 A.M.–4:30 P.M.
daily.

TASTINGS: $10 for 4 or
5 wines.

TOURS: None.

THE WINES: Cabernet
Sauvignon, Merlot, Petite
Sirah, Sauvignon Blanc.

SPECIALTY: Bee Bee's Blend
(Merlot blend).

WINEMAKER: Nils Venge.

ANNUAL PRODUCTION:
1,800 cases.

OF SPECIAL NOTE:
A picnic area beside tasting
room features views of the
Palisades. Also in view of
the winery is Old Faithful
Geyser and an old home
featured in the Hugh
Grant movie *Nine Months*.
Annual events include
Calistoga Wineries Spring
Celebration (May). Two
other labels are available
at Envy: Vine Haven wines
(Chardonnay, Merlot, and
Rosé) and Carter Cellars
wines.

NEARBY ATTRACTIONS:
Old Faithful Geyser
of California; Petrified
Forest (walking trails
through Pliocene fossil
forest formed by volcanic
action); Robert Louis
Stevenson State Park
(hiking).

What's the story behind the name of this winery? Why Envy? According to cofounder Mark Carter, he and partner Nils Venge considered calling it simply NV. That would be catchy, with its clever reference to Napa Valley, as well as the term nonvintage, which is applied to wines blended from two or more different years. A trendy restaurant in downtown Napa called itself NV, but it went belly-up after less than two years in business. That didn't seem a good omen. Since many people who visit Napa are envious of the wine country lifestyle, spelling out the name Envy struck the partners as a better option.

Mark Carter, a native Californian who owns two inns and a restaurant in Eureka, gained a reputation in wine circles more  than a decade ago, when his stellar wine list was selected seven years in a row as a recipient of a Grand Award from *Wine Spectator* magazine. Carter went so far as to convert one of the prized rooms in his Hotel Carter into a cellar to accommodate his vast collection of fine vintages.

Carter and Venge crossed paths in the early 1980s when Venge appeared at the hotelier's very first winemaker dinner. By then, Nils Venge was a well-known figure in the Napa Valley and beyond. As a vintner, grape grower, and consultant to many start-up wineries, Venge has been planting, pruning, crushing, fermenting, blending, and bottling in various vineyards and wineries since launching his career at Sterling Vineyards in the early 1970s. In 1976 he established his own label, Saddleback Cellars, which is located off Oakville Cross Road on a little lane called Money Road.

They never dreamed they would wind up as partners in a new wine venture in Calistoga, but by 1998, as Carter tells the story, he convinced Venge to help him produce wines under the Carter Cellars label. The wines they made regularly garnered more than ninety points from the *Wine Enthusiast* and *Wine & Spirits* as well as *Wine Spectator*. The wines, which carried the names of various notable vineyards (including Napa's esteemed To Kalon and Truchard vineyards) on the label, were produced in small lots, mostly between seventy-five and two hundred cases.

Eventually, the hotelier and the wine guru realized it was time to buy land with a vineyard on it. A two-year search of every available piece of property in the Napa Valley led them to a site once occupied by Calistoga Cellars. They bought the existing winery and its adjacent eleven-plus acres of estate vineyards, planted to Cabernet Sauvignon, Merlot, and Petite Sirah. A two-story residential-looking structure washed in ocher now houses Envy's winery and tasting room, which opened in March of 2007.

FAILLA

FAILLA
3530 Silverado Trail North
St. Helena, CA 94574
707-963-0530
info@faillawines.com
www.faillawines.com

OWNERS: Ehren Jordan
and Anne-Marie Failla.

LOCATION: About 4.5 miles
northeast of St. Helena.

APPELLATION: Napa Valley.

HOURS: By appointment,
10 A.M.–5 P.M.

TASTINGS: $10 for 3 or
4 wines.

TOURS: By appointment.

THE WINES: Chardonnay,
Pinot Noir, Syrah, Viognier.

SPECIALTY: Cool-climate
wines.

WINEMAKER: Ehren Jordan.

ANNUAL PRODUCTION:
4,000 cases.

OF SPECIAL NOTE: The
original Silverado Trail
runs through the property.

NEARBY ATTRACTIONS:
Bothe-Napa State Park
(hiking, picnicking, horseback riding, swimming
Memorial Day–Labor
Day); Silverado Museum
(Robert Louis Stevenson
memorabilia); Culinary
Institute of America
at Greystone (cooking
demonstrations).

Sequestered in a forested nook off the Silverado Trail, Failla's hospitality center is as unpretentious as it comes in wine country. The interior of the vintage yellow farmhouse has been transformed into something along the lines of a family fishing lodge, complete with knotty pine walls, hardwood floors, and a stone fireplace. The decor is largely whimsical—paintings of trout, old board games, early Americana signs, and oddities such as a lamp fashioned from weathered croquet balls and mallet heads. Most of the walls are taken up with bookshelves filled with tomes on art, old *National Geographic* magazines, and family memorabilia.

The tasting bar is tucked into a large alcove at the east end of the living room, where a curved swath of redwood rests on top of upended wine barrels. Guests like to take a seat on a nearby sofa or club chair, where they can examine the wines at leisure.

Ehren Jordan and Anne-Marie Failla (pronounced "FAY-la") founded the winery in 1998, having taken very circuitous routes to become winery owners. Failla was involved in investment banking in New York and Tokyo, in venture capital in Boston and the Bay Area, and then in the Internet start-up business in San Francisco  before being lured by her future husband to the Napa Valley, where she worked at Beringer Wine Estates and Chappellet Vineyards. Jordan's path was even more peripatetic, including stints as a ski bum and a sales rep for a large wine distributor. Eventually he drifted to Napa and was hired at Joseph Phelps Vineyards, where he learned the ropes from Bruce Neyers, then vice president. After that, it was off to France and the venerable vineyards of the Rhône Valley.

Upon his return to the United States in 1994, Jordan joined Bruce Neyers as winemaking partner at Neyers Vineyards in St. Helena and then was hired by Larry Turley, for whom he still works today as winemaker at the highly respected Turley Wine Cellars on California's Central Coast. When Jordan saw Turley's estate vineyards on the Sonoma Coast, he was struck by the Rhône-like conditions and inspired to buy eighty acres, eleven of which later became Failla's estate vineyard planted to Chardonnay, Syrah, and Pinot Noir.

It would be several more years before Ehren Jordan would have his own winery. In 2004 he and Failla purchased ten acres that included the old farmhouse and a late nineteenth-century stone winery that had once served as a mill for producing hard apple cider. In due course, he will start replacing most of the five-acre apple orchard with vines. For the 2008 harvest, he debuted a twelve-thousand-square-foot cave with a bi-level fermentation room featuring gravity-flow wine movement.

FLORA SPRINGS WINERY & VINEYARDS

This winery's history is a cautionary tale of sorts: Be careful what you wish for. In 1977 Jerry and Flora Komes were looking for a place to relax and watch the grapes grow. Their search led them to the Napa Valley, which has countless porches with vineyard views. Even then, they weren't thinking of growing the grapes themselves, let alone making wine.

Then the couple saw the 1956 Louis M. Martini house in the western foothills. Louis had died three years previously, and the property was looking rather shabby. Two of the buildings, the 1888 Rennie Winery and the 1885 Charles Brockhoff Winery, were filled with bats, rats, and rattlesnakes. The place looked more like a ghost town than a potential residence, but it had the key ingredient: the very views that Jerry and Flora Komes desired. As Jerry recalled, "Outside of a home, it had all the things we weren't looking for."

The couple bought the package and, inspired by the legacy of the land, decided to restore the property. Like so many other retirement projects, this one became a consuming passion that threatened the prospect of leisurely afternoons rocking on the porch. Before long, the property served as a magnet, luring two of Jerry and Flora's children. Son John, a general contractor and home winemaker, was fascinated by the challenges of producing wine and breathing life into the aged buildings. Daughter Julie and her husband, Pat Garvey, gave up careers in education, and Pat dedicated himself to learning the grape-growing business. Another son, Mike, also became a partner. After two vintages, John decided that he and Julie had pressed their luck as winemakers to the limit, so Ken Deis was hired in 1980. In 2008 he passed the winemaking baton to his assistant of eighteen years, Paul Steinauer.

John's wife, Carrie, gets the credit for naming the winery. There were two obvious life-giving sources to this venture, Flora Komes herself and the continuously flowing springs that were the sole source of water for the property. Flora Springs had almost immediate success. The first commercially released wine, a Chardonnay, won a gold medal at the prestigious Los Angeles County Fair, the beginning of many awards and much critical acclaim for the winery.

Over the years, the family has acquired 650 acres of vineyards in nine distinct Napa Valley locations, in addition to the original Komes Ranch. The winery sells 80 percent of these grapes to twenty-five premium wineries, which gives Flora Springs a unique opportunity to select the 20 percent that fits the winery's criteria. Visitors may sample the Flora Springs wines daily at the tasting room or make an appointment to tour the winery.

FLORA SPRINGS WINERY & VINEYARDS
Tasting Room:
677 St. Helena Hwy. South
St. Helena, CA 94574
707-967-8032
Winery:
1978 W. Zinfandel Ln.
St. Helena, CA 94574
707-963-5711
info@florasprings.com
www.florasprings.com

OWNERS: Komes and Garvey families.

LOCATION: About 1 mile south of downtown St. Helena (tasting room).

APPELLATION: Napa Valley.

HOURS: 10 A.M.–5 P.M. daily (tasting room).

TASTINGS: $15–$35 for various tastings.

TOURS: Of winery by appointment (707-967-6723).

THE WINES: Chardonnay, Merlot, Pinot Grigio, Sangiovese, Single-vineyard Cabernet Sauvignons, Soliloquy (Sauvignon Blanc), Trilogy (Meritage).

SPECIALTY: Soliloquy, Trilogy.

WINEMAKER: Paul Steinauer.

ANNUAL PRODUCTION: 45,000 cases.

OF SPECIAL NOTE: Picnic tables available at tasting room.

NEARBY ATTRACTIONS: Bothe-Napa State Park (hiking, picnicking, swimming Memorial Day–Labor Day); Culinary Institute of America at Greystone (cooking demonstrations).

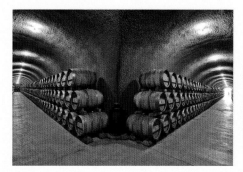

FRANK FAMILY VINEYARDS

FRANK FAMILY VINEYARDS
1091 Larkmead Ln.
Calistoga, CA 94515
800-574-9463
www.frankfamily
vineyards.com

OWNERS: Frank family (Rich, Connie, Paul, Darryl, Vanessa, Lewis, Stella, and Jeremy).

LOCATION: About 5 miles north of St. Helena via Hwy. 29.

APPELLATION: Napa Valley.

HOURS: 10 A.M.–5 P.M. daily.

TASTINGS: Complimentary.

TOURS: By appointment.

THE WINES: Cabernet Sauvignon, Chardonnay, Pinot Noir, Sangiovese, sparkling wine, Zinfandel.

SPECIALTIES: Cabernet Sauvignon from Rutherford, Chardonnay, sparkling wine.

WINEMAKER: Todd Graff.

ANNUAL PRODUCTION: 20,000 cases.

OF SPECIAL NOTE: Carneros Chardonnay; Reserve Chardonnay, Pinot Noir, Sangiovese and Zinfandel; Rutherford Reserve Cabernet; Winston Hill Red Wine; and *méthode champenoise* sparkling wines available only at winery.

NEARBY ATTRACTIONS: Bothe-Napa State Park; Robert Louis Stevenson State Park; Old Faithful Geyser of California; Petrified Forest; hot-air balloon rides; Sharpsteen Museum (exhibits on Robert Louis Stevenson and Walt Disney animator Ben Sharpsteen).

At a time when many Napa Valley wineries are increasingly exclusive, the convivial, unpretentious ambience at Frank Family Vineyards is decidedly refreshing. What's more, the winery bucks another local trend by offering complimentary tastings. Yet these are not the main reasons for heading slightly off the beaten path to reach this historic property. The Frank Family Vineyards wines are made in a massive stone building first constructed in 1884 as Larkmead Winery. Refurbished in 1906 with sandstone from the nearby hills, the structure is listed on the National Register of Historic Places and as an official Point of Historical Interest in the state of California.

In 1992 Rich Frank, former president of Disney Studios, had the opportunity to purchase the Kornell Champagne Cellars at Larkmead Winery. A sentimental guy at heart, Frank continues to produce sparkling wines in the old cellar where thick stone walls, high-stacked barrels, and the unmistakable bouquet of aging wines impart an almost palpable sense of history. Winemaker Todd Graff, who was previously a winemaker at Schramsberg, handcrafts Blanc de Blancs, Blanc de Noirs, Rouge, and Reserve in the traditional French *méthode champenoise* style. Visitors can see the equipment Graff uses to produce 2,200 cases of sparkling wine each year.

The focus at Frank Family Vineyards, however, is largely on still wines, using grapes from three distinguished Napa vineyards. Winston Hill, Rich Frank's personal estate, is situated five hundred feet above the valley floor in Rutherford and produces Cabernet Sauvignon as well as small amounts of Merlot, Cabernet Franc, and Sangiovese. The grapes from this vineyard are used for Frank Family's estate wines—Winston Hill Red Wine, Rutherford Reserve Cabernet, and Rutherford Reserve Sangiovese. Fruit for the winery's Napa Valley Cabernet Sauvignon also comes from the SJ Vineyard in the Capell Valley, located east of the Vaca Range. Frank Family's Lewis Vineyard at Buchli Station is in the heart of Carneros, where the combination of cool maritime climate and shallow, dense clay loam soils produces lively, well-balanced Chardonnay and Pinot Noir.

As former president of Disney Studios, Rich Frank knows how to make visitors feel welcome. The tasting room, at times brimming with laughter, is recognized among the best in the country—the May 2008 *Wine Enthusiast* included it as one of only six Napa wineries awarded a spot on the list of the country's top twenty-five tasting rooms. A new room, in a remodeled Craftsman house on the property, provides separate areas for sampling sparkling wines and still wines. Outside, visitors are welcome to relax at the wooden picnic tables and enjoy the spectacular vineyard views.

1091 LARKMEAD LANE

FRANK FAMILY
VINEYARDS

AT

THE HISTORIC LARKMEAD WINERY
ESTABLISHED 1884

POINT OF
HISTORICAL
INTEREST

GRGICH HILLS ESTATE

Few people driving along Highway 29 recognize both of the red, white, and blue flags flying in front of this winery. They certainly know one, the American flag. The other represents Croatia, the native country of winemaker and co-owner Miljenko "Mike" Grgich.

The simple red-tile-roofed, white stucco building may not be as flashy as those of nearby wineries, but as the saying goes, it's what's inside that counts. Once visitors pass beneath the grapevine trellis and into the dimly lit recesses of the tasting room, they forget about exterior appearances. The comfortable, old-world atmosphere at Grgich Hills Estate is not a gimmick.

The winery was founded by Mike Grgich (pronounced "GUR-gitch") and Austin E. Hills on July 4, 1977. Both were already well known. Hills is a member of the Hills Brothers coffee family. Grgich was virtually legend-ary, especially in France. He had drawn worldwide attention in 1976, when, at the now-famous "Paris Tasting," an all-French panel of judges chose his 1973 Chateau Montelena Chardonnay over the best of the white Burgundies in a blind tasting. It was a momentous occasion for the California wine industry in general and in particular for Mike Grgich, who was already acknowledged as one of the state's top winemakers.

Finally in a position to capitalize on his fame, Grgich quickly found a simpatico partner in Hills, who had a background in business and finance and was the owner of established vineyards. The two men shortly began turning out the intensely flavored Chardonnays that remain the flagship wines of Grgich Hills Estate.

Grgich, easily recognizable with his trademark blue beret, was born in 1923 into a winemaking family on the Dalmatian coast of Croatia. He arrived in California in 1958 and spent his early years at Beaulieu Vineyard, where he worked with the late, pioneering winemaker André Tchelistcheff before moving on to Mondavi and Chateau Montelena. Grgich continues to make wine and relies on a younger generation—daughter Violet Grgich, vice president of sales and marketing, and nephew Ivo Jeramaz, vice president of production and vineyard development—to carry on the family tradition. Visitors may well run into family members when taking the exceptionally informative winery tour or while sampling wines in the cool, cellarlike tasting room or in the VIP tasting room and hospitality center.

GRGICH HILLS ESTATE
1829 St. Helena Hwy.
Rutherford, CA 94573
800-532-3057
info@grgich.com
www.grgich.com

OWNERS: Miljenko "Mike" Grgich and Austin Hills.

LOCATION: About 3 miles south of St. Helena.

APPELLATION: Napa Valley.

HOURS: 9:30 A.M.–4:30 P.M. daily.

TASTINGS: $10 for 5 wines.

TOURS: By appointment, 11 A.M. and 2 P.M. daily.

THE WINES: Cabernet Sauvignon, Chardonnay, Fumé Blanc, Merlot, Violetta (late-harvest dessert wine), Zinfandel.

SPECIALTY: Chardonnay.

WINEMAKER: Mike Grgich.

ANNUAL PRODUCTION: 70,000 cases.

OF SPECIAL NOTE: Barrel tastings held 2–4 P.M. on Friday afternoons, except during harvest, when grape stomping is offered daily. Napa Valley Wine Train stops at Grgich Hills for special tour and tasting; call 800-427-4124 for schedule.

NEARBY ATTRACTIONS: Bothe-Napa State Park (hiking, picnicking, horseback riding, swimming Memorial Day–Labor Day); Bale Grist Mill State Historic Park (water-powered mill circa 1846); Silverado Museum (Robert Louis Stevenson memorabilia).

HALL ST. HELENA

HALL ST. HELENA
401 St. Helena Hwy. South
St. Helena, CA 94574
707-967-0700
celebrate@hallwines.com
www.hallwines.com

OWNERS: Craig and
Kathryn Hall.

LOCATION: 2 miles south of
St. Helena.

APPELLATION: Napa Valley.

HOURS: 10 A.M.–5:30 P.M.
daily.

TASTINGS: $15 for 3 or
4 wines; $25 for 2 reserve
wines.

TOURS: By appointment at
11 A.M., 1 P.M., and 3 P.M.
daily and includes barrel
tasting ($30).

THE WINES: Cabernet
Sauvignon, Merlot,
Sauvignon Blanc.

SPECIALTY: Bordeaux
varietals.

WINEMAKER: Steve Leveque.

ANNUAL PRODUCTION:
40,000 cases.

OF SPECIAL NOTE: Winery
displays owners' collection
of contemporary art. A
number of picnic areas
available in a mulberry
tree–shaded arbor
adjacent to the tasting
room.

NEARBY ATTRACTIONS:
Bothe-Napa State Park
(hiking, picnicking,
horseback riding,
swimming Memorial
Day–Labor Day); Bale
Grist Mill State Historic
Park (water-powered mill
circa 1846); Silverado
Museum (Robert Louis
Stevenson memorabilia).

V intners Craig and Kathryn Hall are the kind of people who dream big—and then bring those dreams to life in dramatic fashion. Kathryn Hall had long wanted a chance to continue her family's winemaking heritage and grabbed the opportunity to take over an existing winery that, despite its historic significance, was largely overlooked by wine lovers. Her goal was to become known as a seriously dedicated boutique producer of Bordeaux varietals that would express the true character of both the fruit and the land.

After buying an existing property, which included a tasting room as well as an adjacent winemaking facility dating to 1885, the Halls in 2003 opened Hall St. Helena, an expression of their personal vision and a connoisseur's mastery of hospitality and artistic appreciation. They transformed a lackluster tasting room into a destination not only for wine aficionados but also for fans of modern art. The twenty-year-old structure is now an airy, colorful space further brightened by original artwork from the Halls' own collection. As a sign of great things to come, the tasting room's entrance courtyard is dominated by

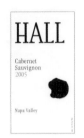

a seven-foot-tall sculpture, *Moebus Tower*, in the shape of a horizontal figure eight, the symbol of infinity. Painted a vibrant red, the piece inspired the color of the winery's logo. Hall St. Helena also commissioned a number of wine-related sculptures that adorn the grounds.

That commitment is best conveyed in the wines: Cabernet Sauvignon, Merlot, and Sauvignon Blanc. The Halls own nearly 3,300 acres in Napa and Sonoma valleys, nearly 500 of which are planted to grapevines. (A second winery, Hall Rutherford, is open only by appointment.)

Hall St. Helena, open daily to the public, offers a tour of the original 1885 winery that concludes with a barrel tasting of the most recent vintages, together with a sit-down reserve tasting of currently released bottled wines. Located next door to the tasting room, the historic stone structure was built by New England sea captain William Peterson, the first of several owners over the next century.

The winery's history may be rich, but it is what lies in the future that has the wine world excited. The Halls have commissioned renowned architect Frank Gehry to design a state-of-the-art gravity-flow winery. The new buildings will incorporate sustainable, energy-efficient design in keeping with the U.S. Green Building Council's certification regulations. Already, visitors can make an appointment for a guided tour that culminates with a formal tasting in the Gehry Gallery, a display of the architect's models and plans. These tours showcase not only the visionary future of Hall St. Helena but the Bordeaux varietal wines that the Halls set out to create from the very beginning.

HARTWELL VINEYARDS

The setting at Hartwell Vineyards is more than worthy of any hilltop villa in the Italian wine country. Perched on a knoll at the crest of a winding driveway, the winery commands a regal view of vineyards and the dramatic rock outcroppings that characterize the prestigious Stags Leap appellation. Venerable oak trees shade the landscaped approach, while closer to the entrance, deep green, columnar cypress trees punctuate the monochromatic expanse of the winery's smooth ocher facade. Although the structure was completed only in 1998, its Tuscan-inspired architecture further evokes the European countryside.

Invisible from the public road and accessed by a private gate, the estate is off-limits except by appointment, but once inside, guests are treated like royalty. On the other side of enormous arched pine doors, visits begin with a welcoming glass of Sauvignon Blanc in the foyer. Tours progress seamlessly as a host moves through the winery and into the 5,000-square-foot caves, ushering guests into the domed Star Tasting Room. In this secluded space, some forty-five feet underground, everyone is seated in upholstered straight-back chairs around an octagonal table set on top of an antique wagon wheel. The Hartwells bought the piece from Harry See of See's Candy fame, who used to own the property. And speaking of "stars," as unlikely as it might seem, the wheel appeared in one of Ronald Reagan's commercials for Borax in the 1960s.

If the room has a theme, it is eclecticism: A metal fireplace used to belong to George Yount, the pioneering grape grower for whom nearby Yountville was named. A pair of brass stags is set on a curvilinear marble-topped credenza with wrought-iron legs, and an oil-on-fabric painting represents the gateway to vineyards. Surrounded by collectibles and textured, mustard-colored walls, groups are served a course of artisan cheeses from around the world paired with four Hartwell wines. Afterward, a barrel tasting paired with chocolate truffles from Anette's Chocolates in downtown Napa is held in the sales salon. Burgundy sofas and chairs with gilded armrests provide comfortable seating, and old photographs of Robert Hartwell's collection of Porsches and other classic automobiles add visual interest.

Hartwell was a successful businessman in Southern California when he became enamored of Napa wines. In 1985, when the area where he had lived most of his life became too crowded, he embarked on a quest for a vineyard, which led him to an uncleared property in the Stags Leap District. Hartwell began planting vines in the rich volcanic soil of the appellation known for terrain that produces intensely flavored grapes and in 1997 started construction on the winery.

HARTWELL VINEYARDS
5795 Silverado Trail
Napa, CA 94558
800-366-6516
info@hartwellvineyards.com
www.hartwellvineyards.com

OWNERS: Robert and Blanca Hartwell.

LOCATION: Between Oak Knoll Ave. and Yountville Cross Rd.

APPELLATION: Stags Leap District.

HOURS: By appointment, Monday–Saturday.

TASTINGS: $25 for 4 wines; $45 for a flight of wines paired with imported cheeses.

TOURS: Included with wine-and-cheese pairing.

THE WINES: Cabernet Sauvignon, Merlot, Sauvignon Blanc.

SPECIALTY: Limited-production estate wines.

WINEMAKER: Benoit Touquette (consulting winemaker: Michel Rolland).

ANNUAL PRODUCTION: 3,000–4,000 cases.

OF SPECIAL NOTE: Hillside vineyards planted atop a dormant 4-million-year-old volcano. Late Harvest Cabernet Sauvignon available only at winery.

NEARBY ATTRACTIONS: Napa Valley Museum (winemaking displays, art exhibits).

HEITZ WINE CELLARS

HEITZ WINE CELLARS
Tasting Room:
436 St. Helena Hwy. South
St. Helena, CA 94574
Winery:
500 Taplin Rd.
St. Helena, CA 94574
707-963-3542
www.heitzcellar.com

OWNERS: Heitz family.

LOCATION: 2 miles south of
St. Helena (tasting room).

APPELLATION: Napa Valley.

HOURS: 11 A.M.–4:30 P.M.
daily (tasting room).

TASTINGS: Complimentary.

TOURS: Of winery by
appointment.

THE WINES: Cabernet
Sauvignon, Chardonnay,
Grignolino, Grignolino
Rosé, Port, Sauvignon
Blanc, Zinfandel.

SPECIALTIES: Vineyard-
designated Cabernet
Sauvignons (Bella Oaks
Vineyard, Martha's
Vineyard, Trailside
Vineyard).

WINEMAKERS: David Heitz,
Joe Norman.

ANNUAL PRODUCTION:
40,000 cases.

OF SPECIAL NOTE: Only
producer of Italian variety
of Grignolino in Napa
Valley. Limited production
of Petit Verdot available
only in tasting room.

NEARBY ATTRACTIONS:
Bothe-Napa State Park
(hiking, picnicking, horseback riding, swimming
Memorial Day–Labor
Day); Culinary Institute
of America at Greystone
(cooking demonstrations);
Silverado Museum
(Robert Louis Stevenson
memorabilia).

Most travelers interested in sampling Heitz wines will visit the tasting room on Highway 29, the original site of the winery founded in 1961 by Joe and Alice Heitz. Palms, traditional symbols of hospitality, greet visitors turning off the highway toward the native-stone building that opened in 2002. Inside, the mahogany floors, cabinets, and long, low tasting bar make for a sophisticated space. Behind the tasting room is a patio with ample bench seating in the shade of a pergola. Just fifteen feet beyond it are the very first vineyards planted by the Heitzes.

Today, a second generation is in charge of Heitz Wine Cellars: president Kathleen Heitz Myers and her brother, winemaker David Heitz. David has earned accolades beginning with his first solo effort, in 1974. No one was surprised by his success, since David learned the wine business at the knee of his father, one of the most influential winemakers of his time. The late Joe Heitz honed his craft at a few wineries, notably Beaulieu Vineyard, where he spent seven years as understudy to acclaimed winemaker André Tchelistcheff.

It didn't take Joe and Alice Heitz long to outgrow their 8-acre property. In 1964 they relocated two miles east, to a 160-acre residence and ranch on Taplin Road, a tiny country road in an area known locally as Spring Valley. The original winery became the first tasting room, then was replaced by the structure visitors see today. The Taplin Road property had first been developed as a winery and vineyard in the 1880s by the Swiss-Italian family of Anton Rossi. Old oaks, rosebushes, wisteria, shaded benches, a couple of small farmhouses, and a beautiful 1898 stone cellar make parts of the ranch look more like a movie set than a working winery. Today, the Heitz family farms a total of 370 acres of vineyards at their various Napa Valley ranches.

The most famous wines Heitz makes come from three prestigious Napa Valley Cabernet vineyards: Martha's Vineyard, Trailside Vineyard, and Bella Oaks Vineyard. Perhaps no other vineyard name in the United States is as widely recognized as Martha's Vineyard in Oakville. Owned by the Tom and Martha May family, the thirty-four-acre property produces Cabernet Sauvignon known for its minty characteristics, rich flavors, and overall balance.

Like their parents before them, Kathleen Heitz Myers and David Heitz place a high premium on preserving the agricultural heritage of the Napa Valley. They practice sustainable and organic farming, which not only creates healthier vines but ensures that the distinct characteristics of each vineyard are expressed in the complexities of the wine. Heitz Wine Cellars was one of the earliest to enroll in Napa County's Green Program, which works to safeguard the Napa River watershed.

THE HESS COLLECTION WINERY

A gently winding road heads up a forested mountainside to this winery on the western rim of the Napa Valley. Although only a fifteen-minute drive from bustling Highway 29, the estate feels a thousand times removed. Arriving visitors are greeted with stunning vineyard views from almost every vantage point.

Swiss entrepreneur Donald Hess has owned vineyards on Mount Veeder since 1978, so when he decided to establish his own winery, he didn't have to look far to find the Christian Brothers Mont La Salle property. He already knew that the east side of the extinct volcano provides a cool climate that allows a long growing season as well as excellent soil drainage—two viticultural components known for producing Cabernet Sauvignon with excellent structure and superb concentration of aromas and flavors. Vineyards were first planted on this land in the 1860s, long before the three-story, ivy-clad stone winery was built in 1903. The Christian Brothers produced wine here for nearly a half century before leasing the facilities to Hess in 1986. He began planting Cabernet Sauvignon vineyards on terrain so steep they have to be picked by hand. The vines must grow extended roots to cling to the mountainside, and the resultant stress creates fruit of exceptional character.

The Hess Collection farms 310 acres of Mount Veeder vineyards that range in elevation from six hundred to two thousand feet. Viewing itself as a steward of the land, the winery farms these vineyards using the principles of sustainable and organic agriculture.

Hess spent three years renovating the facility before opening it to the public in 1989. The overhaul included transforming thirteen thousand square feet on the second and third floors to display his extensive collection of international art, which includes 143 paintings, sculptures, and interactive pieces by modern and contemporary artists including such luminaries as Francis Bacon, Frank Stella, Anselm Kiefer, Andy Goldsworthy, and Robert Motherwell. Two works evoke a particularly strong response for their social commentary. One is Argentinean Leopold Maler's *Hommage 1974*, an eternally burning typewriter created in protest of the repression of artistic freedom. Another is Polish sculptor Magdalena Abakanowicz's *Crowd*, a group of nineteen life-size headless figures made of resin and burlap sacks.

The tasting room, which shares the first floor with a century-old barrel-aging cellar, is built from a local metamorphic sandstone called rhyolite. The stone had been covered with stucco by the Christian Brothers but was inadvertently exposed during the winery's renovation. This is where visitors linger and share their impressions of both the wine and the art.

THE HESS COLLECTION WINERY
4411 Redwood Rd.
Napa, CA 94558
707-255-8584
www.hesscollection.com

FOUNDER: Donald Hess.

LOCATION: 7 miles west of Hwy. 29.

APPELLATIONS: Mount Veeder, Napa Valley.

HOURS: 10 A.M.–5:30 P.M. daily in summer; 10 A.M.– 5 P.M. daily in winter.

TASTINGS: $10–$20. Food-and-wine pairings at 10 A.M. and 2 P.M. on Thursday, Friday, and Saturday by reservation.

TOURS: Art collection open daily. Guided tours of winery and collection available.

THE WINES: Cabernet Sauvignon, Chardonnay, 19 Block Cuvée, Petite Sirah, Sauvignon Blanc, Viognier, Zinfandel.

SPECIALTIES: Mount Veeder Cabernet Sauvignon, Chardonnay, 19 Block Cuvée.

WINEMAKERS: David Guffy (Hess), Randle Johnson (Artezin).

ANNUAL PRODUCTION: 90,000 cases.

OF SPECIAL NOTE: Extensive collection of international art. Many wines available only in tasting room.

NEARBY ATTRACTIONS: COPIA: The American Center for Wine, Food and the Arts; Alston Regional Park (hiking).

JOSEPH PHELPS VINEYARDS

JOSEPH PHELPS VINEYARDS
200 Taplin Rd.
St. Helena, CA 94574
707-967-3720
jpvwines@jpvwines.com
www.jpvwines.com

OWNER: Joseph Phelps.

LOCATION: .25 mile east
of Silverado Trail between
Zinfandel Ln. and Pope St.

APPELLATION: Napa Valley.

HOURS: 9 A.M.–4 P.M.
Monday–Friday; 10 A.M.–
4 P.M. Saturday–Sunday.

TASTINGS: By appointment;
$20 for 6 wines.

TOURS: None.

THE WINES: Cabernet
Sauvignon, Eisrebe, Insignia
(Bordeaux-style blend),
Le Mistral (red wine blend),
Sauvignon Blanc, Syrah,
Viognier.

SPECIALTY: Insignia.

WINEMAKERS: Damian
Parker, Ashley Hepworth.

ANNUAL PRODUCTION:
75,000 cases.

OF SPECIAL NOTE: Tastings
and in-depth seminars
available at varying prices.
Picnic tables available by
reservation (no food sold
on premises).

NEARBY ATTRACTIONS:
Bothe-Napa State Park
(hiking, picnicking,
horseback riding,
swimming Memorial
Day–Labor Day); Bale Grist
Mill State Historic Park
(water-powered mill circa
1846); Silverado Museum
(Robert Louis Stevenson
memorabilia).

The approach to this imposing redwood structure leads up a long, gently sloped driveway that crests a knoll before ending near the winery. Visitors enter via a breezeway beneath an enormous trellis fashioned from century-old bridge ties and draped with wisteria vines that rise from a bed of ivy constantly misted with water from invisible fountains. The reception area is to the left, but straight ahead is a compelling, panoramic view of vineyards, the winery's lake to the north, and mountains on the western horizon. It is hard to resist continuing through the breezeway to the wide terrace beyond. There, low stone walls offer a resting place where people can sit and take in the vista of grapevines that extend from the winery westward as if they were going to climb right up the slopes of the majestic Mayacamas Range in the distance.

The terrace at Joseph Phelps Vineyards is as hospitable a setting as can be found anywhere in wine country. It is the ideal  spot, especially on a sunny afternoon, to soak up the ambience of a hidden slice of heaven known as Spring Valley. Once a sprawling cattle ranch, the 600-acre property encompasses rolling terrain, 130 acres of grapevines, and a sprinkling of valley oaks. Within view of the terrace is a new grove of olive trees, four acres of Tuscan varieties that produce the fruit for the winery's private-label extra-virgin olive oil.

The olive trees and their oil are emblematic of the winery's increased emphasis on organic practices. At certain times of year, 150 ewes and baby lambs can be seen meandering the vineyards, part of a lease-a-sheep program that allows the animals to feed on the grass and other vegetation that sprouts among the rows of vines. After bud break each spring, the herd is moved out, lest they nibble on the precious grapes-to-be. The winery also avails itself of chickens (housed in portable coops) and wild turkeys that eat insects and provide natural fertilizer. Joseph Phelps Vineyards is also home to a number of beehives (for pollination and honey production) managed by the assistant vineyard manager.

Not all the animals here are put to work: jackrabbits bound around the vineyards, and dozens of quail and their offspring can often be seen scooting about the thicket that grows along the front wall of the terrace.

On the far side of the thicket are the Cabernet Sauvignon vineyards that have been the winery's major focus since its founding in 1972. Joseph Phelps Vineyards' specialty is Insignia, a pioneering, proprietary blend of the highest quality Napa Valley Cabernet Sauvignon and other Bordeaux grape varieties from 100 percent estate vineyards.

KULETO ESTATE

Built on virgin land less than twenty years ago, the Tuscan-style villa and winery at the pinnacle of this 761-acre estate could be mistaken for a rustic village perched on an Italian hilltop. In 1992, after culinary entrepreneur Pat Kuleto assembled five parcels from cattle ranchers, he set out to create a serene and sustainable retreat where he could indulge his passion for fine food and wine. An equally important goal was to foster European-style hospitality that would entice friends and wine lovers to the scenic property overlooking Lake Hennessey, Pritchard Hill, and the towns of Rutherford and St. Helena.

Erecting buildings, along with a swimming pool, on relatively flat ground was one thing, but planting grapevines on wild, steep terrain would be quite another. Famed in the food world for fashioning memorable restaurants out Kuleto was undeterred when faced with vineyards on Napa Valley's eastern

of previously unremarkable spaces, the challenge of creating world-class mountains.

As Kuleto explored his new surthe manzanita scrub, chaparral, and trum of distinct soil types and individa remarkable range of grape varietals. the land, he would have to establish roundings, he discovered that beneath spindly madrone saplings was a special environments that would support Kuleto realized that, due to the lay of separate terraced lots and choose the rootstocks and clones best suited to each location and orientation. Within a year, he began planting the first wave of varietals, including Cabernet Sauvignon, Chardonnay, Pinot Noir, and Sangiovese. Later would come Muscat, Syrah, Zinfandel, and a handful of other small-lot blending varietals in vineyards established at elevations ranging from 800 to 1,450 feet.

While the grapevines took root and began to mature, Kuleto pursued other aspects of his grand vision for transforming this secluded aerie into a working ranch. He planted fruit orchards and an extensive organic garden and also acquired a menagerie of pigs, goats, ducks, turkeys, rabbits, sheep, and cattle. He established ponds around the property and stocked them with sturgeon, catfish, bluegill, and other fish. In all, the estate probably could feed an entire village.

By 2001 construction was completed on the stone-clad winery, designed by Kuleto to blend in with the old-world look of Villa Cucina, his nearby residence. The 17,000-square-foot, gravity-flow facility may look weathered, but it has all the elements winemaker Dave Lattin needs to craft the lots of ultrapremium fruit from each small vineyard block at every stage of development into wine. Visitors can sample the finished product on a covered verandah overlooking the rolling hillsides studded with oaks and madrones.

KULETO ESTATE
2470 Sage Canyon Rd.
St. Helena, CA 94574
707-963-9750
info@kuletoestate.com
www.kuletoestate.com

OWNER: Pat Kuleto.

LOCATION: About 10.5 miles southeast of St. Helena.

APPELLATION: Napa Valley.

HOURS: By appointment only.

TASTINGS: Part of tour fee.

TOURS: By appointment, 10:30 A.M., 11:45 A.M., 1 P.M., and 2:30 P.M. daily. Fee ($35) includes tour, 4 wine samples, and artisan cheese pairing.

THE WINES: Cabernet Franc, Cabernet Sauvignon, Chardonnay, Pinot Noir, Rosato, Sangiovese, Syrah, Zinfandel.

SPECIALTY: Cabernet Sauvignon.

WINEMAKER: Dave Lattin.

ANNUAL PRODUCTION: 8,000 cases.

OF SPECIAL NOTE: The tour features a guided walk around the property with its expansive views of Lake Hennessey. Cabernet Franc, Chardonnay, and Pinot Noir available only at winery.

NEARBY ATTRACTIONS: Lake Hennessey (boating, fishing, camping).

MARKHAM VINEYARDS

MARKHAM VINEYARDS
2812 St. Helena Hwy. North
St. Helena, CA 94574
707-963-5292
www.markhamvineyards.com

OWNER:
Mercian Corporation.

LOCATION: 1 mile north of St. Helena on Hwy. 29.

APPELLATION: Napa Valley.

HOURS: 10 A.M.–5 P.M. daily.

TASTINGS: $10–$20 for current releases and library and estate selections.

TOURS: By appointment.

THE WINES: Cabernet Sauvignon, Chardonnay, Merlot, Sauvignon Blanc.

SPECIALTY: Merlot.

WINEMAKER: Kimberlee Jackson Nicholls.

ANNUAL PRODUCTION: 100,000 cases.

OF SPECIAL NOTE: Visitor center, home of the Harley Bruce Markham Gallery, hosts ongoing exhibits. Group events and dinners in the historic stone cellar by appointment.

NEARBY ATTRACTIONS: Bothe-Napa State Park (hiking, picnicking, horseback riding, swimming Memorial Day–Labor Day); Bale Grist Mill State Historic Park (water-powered mill circa 1846); Culinary Institute of America at Greystone (cooking demonstrations); Silverado Museum (Robert Louis Stevenson memorabilia).

Few people are surprised to hear that Charles Krug, Schramsberg, and Sutter Home wineries were in business in 1874. Less widely known is that they were the only three wineries operating in the Napa Valley that year, when Jean Laurent founded the St. Helena winery that, less than a century later, would become known as Markham Vineyards.

Laurent, a Frenchman from Bordeaux, arrived in California in 1852, drawn by the lure of the 1849 Gold Rush. When his prospecting failed to pan out, he made his way to the city of Napa in 1868 and began growing vegetables. Laurent quickly assessed the high quality of the soil and, being from Bordeaux, realized the Napa Valley was ideally suited to grapevines. Six years later, he established the Laurent Winery in St. Helena. After Laurent died in 1890, the property changed hands a number of times. In 1977 it was purchased by Bruce Markham, who had already acquired prime vineyard land on the Napa Valley floor, including 93 acres in Yountville once owned by Inglenook. By 1978 he had added the Calistoga Ranch at the headlands of the Napa River and the Oak Knoll Vineyard in the Oak Knoll District. Altogether, the Markham estate vineyards now cover 330 acres, including the most recent acquisition, Trubody Vineyards, west of Yountville in the center of the valley. These four areas have distinct microclimates that contribute to the complexity of the various wines produced by the winery.

In 1988 the winery and vineyard holdings were sold to Japan's oldest and largest wine company, Mercian Corporation. Despite these changes, many things have remained constant. The current owners have maintained the winery's dedication to producing ultrapremium wines sold at relatively modest prices. The first employee hired by Markham, Bryan Del Bondio, a native of Napa Valley from a family immersed in winemaking, is now president of Markham Vineyards. Jean Laurent's original stone cellar sits at the heart of the facility.

Stylistically, the winery combines both historic and modern elements, with its old stone and concrete facade, and its subdued red metal roofing supported by round wooden columns. Lily ponds flank the approach to the tasting room, and beyond them, orange and yellow canna lilies provide bursts of color when the plants bloom in spring and summer. The tasting room has a large fireplace to warm visitors on cold days. The Harley Bruce Markham Gallery, named after the winery's founder, features artwork and photography by noted artists.

MUMM NAPA

For connoisseurs of champagne, relaxing outdoors on a sunny day with a glass of bubbly, good friends, and a vineyard view may be the ultimate pleasure. This is obviously what the founders of Mumm Napa had in mind when they conceived of establishing a winery in North America that could produce a sparkling wine that would live up to Champagne standards.

In 1979 representatives of Champagne Mumm of France began quietly searching for the ideal location for a winery. So secretive was their project that they even had a code name for it: Project Lafayette. The point man was  the late Guy Devaux, a native of Epernay, the epicenter of France's Champagne district and an expert on *méthode* *champenoise.* In this French style of winemaking, the wine undergoes its bubble-producing fermentation in the very bottle from which it will be drunk. Devaux crisscrossed the United States for four years before settling on Napa Valley, the country's best-known appellation.

The best way to appreciate Mumm Napa is to start with a tour. The winery has a reputation for putting on one of the best in the business, covering the complicated steps necessary to get all those bubbles into each bottle. The best time of year to take the tour is during the harvest season, usually between mid-August and mid-October. However, there is a lot to see at any time of year, and conveniently, the entire tour takes place on one level.

Visitors enter the winery through the wine shop; the tasting verandah is just beyond, with spectacular views of the vineyards and the Mayacamas Range.

Mumm Napa is also noted for its commitment to fine art photography. The winery exhibits the work of many renowned, as well as local, photographers in its expansive galleries. Guests may explore the Photography Galleries at their leisure, even while they enjoy a glass of sparkling wine. Most notable is the private collection of Mathew Adams, grandson of photographer Ansel Adams, on display in the exhibition gallery.

MUMM NAPA
8445 Silverado Trail
Rutherford, CA 94573
707-967-7700
mumm_info@
mummnapa.com
www.mummnapa.com

OWNER: Pernod Ricard USA.

LOCATION: East of Rutherford, 1 mile south of Rutherford Cross Rd.

APPELLATION: Napa Valley.

HOURS: 10 A.M.–5 P.M. daily.

TASTINGS: $10 and up for flights of 3, or by the flute.

TOURS: Hourly, 10 A.M.–3 P.M.

THE WINES: Blanc de Blancs, Blanc de Noirs, Brut Prestige, Demi Sec, DVX, Sparkling Pinot Noir, Vintage Reserve.

SPECIALTY: Sparkling wine made in traditional French style.

WINEMAKER: Ludovic Dervin.

ANNUAL PRODUCTION: 200,000 cases.

OF SPECIAL NOTE: Exhibits of internationally known and local photographers. Limited availability of Chardonnay, Pinot Gris, and Pinot Noir, and of large-format bottles, at winery.

NEARBY ATTRACTIONS: Napa Valley Museum (winemaking displays, art exhibits).

PATZ & HALL

PATZ & HALL
851 Napa Valley Corporate
Way, Suite A
Napa, CA 94558
877-265-6700
info@patzhall.com
www.patzhall.com

OWNERS: Donald Patz,
Heather Patz, James Hall,
and Anne Moses.

LOCATION: 4 miles south of
downtown Napa.

APPELLATION: Napa Valley.

HOURS: 10 A.M.– 4 P.M.
daily in summer,
Wednesday–Sunday in
winter.

TASTINGS: $40 for 6 wines
paired with food by
advance reservation.

TOURS: None.

THE WINES: Chardonnay,
Pinot Noir.

SPECIALTY: Single-vineyard
designated wines.

WINEMAKER: James Hall.

ANNUAL PRODUCTION:
26,000 cases.

OF SPECIAL NOTE: Patz &
Hall wines are available
for sale at the tasting
bar without advance
reservations during regular
operating hours.

NEARBY ATTRACTIONS:
COPIA: The American
Center for Wine, Food
and the Arts (exhibits,
seminars, tastings, and
gardens); Napa Valley
Wine Train (lunch,
brunch, and dinner
excursions); Napa Valley
Opera House (theatrical
and musical performances
in historic building).

The last place most people would think to look for a well-respected winery's tasting room would be in an anonymous complex of cookie-cutter office buildings. Granted, the exteriors are painted in a sophisticated palette of taupe and mauve. Only when the company's distinguished black and silver logo is close enough to see can visitors feel confident that they have arrived at the Patz & Hall Tasting Salon. The actual winemaking is done elsewhere, miles away on the east side of the town of Sonoma, where Patz & Hall established its own 30,000-square-foot winery in 2007 amid a fast-emerging neighborhood of similar facilities. Prior to that, Patz & Hall wines were produced at other Napa Valley wineries.

Patz & Hall was established in 1988, by four friends—Donald Patz, James Hall, Anne Moses, and Heather Patz—who dedicated themselves to making benchmark wines sourced from distinctive California vineyards. Today, they produce a total of fifteen Chardonnays and Pinot Noirs, all without owning a single vine-yard themselves. Patz & Hall was founded on an unusual business model that began in the 1980s at Flora Springs Winery & Vineyards, when assistant winemaker James Hall and national sales manager Donald Patz forged a close friend-ship. Their mutual enthusiasm for wine produced from elite, small

vineyards inspired them to blend their talents along with those of Anne Moses and Heather Patz. Together, the team boasted a wealth of knowledge and experience gleaned at such prestigious wineries as Far Niente, Girard Winery, and Honig Winery, where Hall was once the winemaker.

The founders apply their specialized expertise and daily attention to different areas of the family-run winery's operations. The cornerstone of Patz & Hall is this integrated, hands-on approach, combined with close personal relationships with growers who supply them with fruit from outstanding family-owned vineyards in the Napa Valley, Russian River Valley, Mendocino County, Sonoma Coast, and Santa Lucia Highlands.

All along, the goal was to have a special place where they could welcome customers and get to know them in person. Opened in 2005 and freshly refurbished in 2008, the Patz & Hall Tasting Salon offers visitors with advance reservations two environments for wine and seasonal food pairings: the tasting bar that was added to the front room and a private salon beyond, where the bustle at most winery tasting rooms seems worlds away. In this secluded space, which is decorated like an exquisite dining room, guided tastings are held at a rectangular table made from reclaimed cherry wood and surrounded by eight chic straight-back chairs covered in a palomino shade of suede. Over the course of an hour or more, guests sample six wines paired with local farmstead cheeses and other light fare.

PEJU

Spotting Peju, even on a winery-lined stretch of Highway 29, is easy, thanks to a fifty-foot-tall tasting tower topped with a distinctive copper roof. Although the tasting tower opened only in late 2003, the structure looks as if it has been there for decades. Like the rest of the property, it could have been transplanted directly from the countryside of southern France.

The Rutherford estate had been producing wine grapes for more than eighty years when Anthony and Herta Peju bought it in 1982. The couple have been improving the thirty-acre property ever since, streamlining vineyard techniques and adding Merlot and Cabernet Franc grapes to the estate's core product, Cabernet Sauvignon. By the mid-1990s, demand for Peju wines outstripped the winery's supply. To satisfy  it, the Pejus acquired a 350-acre property in northern Napa County in the Pope Valley District, planted a variety of grapes, and named it Persephone Vineyard, after a goddess in Greek mythology.

The Pejus entered the wine business by a somewhat circuitous route. Anthony Peju had been living in Europe when he was lured to Los Angeles by the movie industry, but then became interested in horticulture. After he met Herta Behensky, his future wife, he established his own nursery, yet secretly dreamed of owning a farm. The vibrant towns of the Napa Valley and their proximity to San Francisco's cultural attractions enticed him to search for vineyard property. A two-year quest ended in the purchase of what would become Peju Province Winery.

Peju's horticultural experience, combined with his wife's talent for gardening, resulted in two acres of immaculately kept winery gardens. Together, they established a dramatic series of outdoor rooms linked by footpaths and punctuated with fountains and marble sculpture. Hundreds of flowering plants and trees create an aromatic retreat for the Pejus and their visitors. Lining both sides of the driveway are forty-foot-tall sycamore trees, their trunks adorned by gnarled spirals. Visitors reach the tasting room by crossing a small bridge over a pool with fountains. An entrance door of Brazilian cherrywood is carved with the image of a farm girl blending water and wine. Inside the room, three muses gaze down from a century-old stained-glass window. A copper-and-steel railing leads to the mezzanine, where a strategically placed circular window offers a garden view.

Peju remains a small, family-owned winery with two generations working together. Daughters Lisa and Ariana, who joined the family business, have been instrumental in installing solar panels at the winery, earning organic certification at Peju's Rutherford estate, and practicing sustainable farming at the winery's other two properties.

PEJU
8466 Hwy. 29
Rutherford, CA 94573
707-963-3600
800-446-7358
info@peju.com
www.peju.com

OWNERS: Anthony and Herta Peju.

LOCATION: 10 miles north of town of Napa.

APPELLATION: Napa Valley.

HOURS: 10 A.M.–6 P.M. daily.

TASTINGS: $10 (applicable to wine purchase).

TOURS: Self-guided or by appointment.

THE WINES: Cabernet Franc, Cabernet Sauvignon, Chardonnay, Merlot, Provence, Sauvignon Blanc, Syrah, Zinfandel.

SPECIALTIES: Cabernet Franc, H.B. Vineyard Cabernet Sauvignon, Rutherford Reserve Cabernet.

WINEMAKER: Sara Fowler.

ANNUAL PRODUCTION: 35,000 cases.

OF SPECIAL NOTE: Wine-and-food pairings, cooking classes, gift boutique. About 80 percent of wines available only at winery.

NEARBY ATTRACTIONS: Silverado Museum (Robert Louis Stevenson memorabilia); Napa Valley Museum (winemaking displays, art exhibits); Culinary Institute of America at Greystone (cooking demonstrations).

ROBERT MONDAVI WINERY

ROBERT MONDAVI WINERY
7801 Hwy. 29
Oakville, CA 94562
707-259-9463
888-766-6328
info@robertmondavi
winery.com
www.robertmondavi
winery.com

LOCATION: About 16 miles
north of the town of Napa.

APPELLATIONS: Oakville,
Napa Valley.

HOURS: 10 A.M.–5 P.M.
daily.

TASTINGS: $15 for 3 wines
in tasting room (includes
souvenir glass); $30 for
3 wines or à la carte in
To Kalon tasting room.

TOURS: To Kalon tour
every hour by reservation
($25); other tours available
seasonally.

THE WINES: Cabernet
Sauvignon, Chardonnay,
Fumé Blanc, Merlot,
Moscato D'Oro, Pinot
Noir.

SPECIALTIES: Cabernet
Sauvignon Reserve and
Fumé Blanc Reserve.

WINEMAKER:
Genevieve Janssens.

ANNUAL PRODUCTION:
300,000 cases.

OF SPECIAL NOTE: Guided
tastings and food-and-
wine pairings. Cave visits
and picnic area available
by tour only. Large shop
with wine books and
Italian imports. Summer
Festival Concert Series
(July–August); Cabernet
Sauvignon Reserve Release
Party (October).

NEARBY ATTRACTIONS:
COPIA: The American
Center for Wine, Food
and the Arts.

Wineries come and wineries go in the Napa Valley, but in this fast-paced, high-stakes world, few can challenge the lasting achievements of the Robert Mondavi Winery. Since its inception forty years ago, it has remained in the forefront of innovation, from the use of cold fermentation, stainless steel tanks, and small French oak barrels to the collaboration with NASA employing aerial imaging to reveal the health and vigor of grapevines.

Founder Robert Mondavi's cherished goal of producing wines on a par with the best in the world made his name virtually synonymous with California winemaking. That vision is being carried out today with ambitious programs such as the recent To Kalon Project. Named after the historic estate vineyard surrounding the winery, this extensive renovation led to the 2000 unveiling of the To Kalon Fermentation Cellar, which capitalizes on the natural flow of gravity to transport wine through the production system. Although Robert Mondavi pioneered the use of stainless steel fermentation in the 1960s, To Kalon has returned to traditional oak fermentation, based on the belief that the use of oak enhances the aromas, flavors, and complexity of the winery's reserve, district, and vineyard-designated Cabernet Sauvignon.

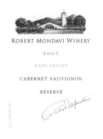

Technological advances aside, the best reason for visiting Robert Mondavi Winery is something less tangible: an opportunity to experience the presentation of wine in the broader context of lifestyle. Educational tours and tastings, concerts, art exhibits, and the industry's first culinary program are all part of the Mondavi legacy. One of the most popular offerings is the To Kalon tour and tasting, which follows the path of the grape from the vine through the cellar to the finished wine. The 550-acre vineyard was named To Kalon (Greek for "the beautiful") by Hamilton Walker Crabb, a winegrowing pioneer who established vineyards here in the late 1800s. It was this property that inspired Robert Mondavi to establish his winery on the site.

Just as the estate's grapes express their *terroir* (the place where they are grown), the winery itself reflects the location and legacy of the Napa Valley. The Spanish mission-style architecture, with its expansive archway and bell tower designed by Clifford May, pays homage to the Franciscan fathers who planted the first grapes in the region. Two long wings project from the open-air lobby to embrace a wide expanse of lawn framed by the Mayacamas Range on the western horizon. Typical of the winery's commitment to the arts, several sculptures by regional artist Beniamino Benvenuto Bufano (who, like Robert Mondavi's family, came from Italy) are displayed in the courtyard and elsewhere around the grounds. In addition, the winery features art exhibits that change every two months.

ROMBAUER VINEYARDS

The quarter-mile-long drive from the Silverado Trail leads to a winery ensconced in a forest of pine trees. On the far side of the low-slung building, a wide California ranch-style porch affords views that extend to the tree-covered ridge of the Mayacamas Range to the southeast. Without another structure in sight, the serene setting has the ambience of a fairy-tale kingdom secluded from the hustle and bustle of the valley floor. Directly below the winery, a gravel path winds down to a hill where roses are planted in the sun and azaleas thrive in the shade. Scattered about are a half-dozen metal sculptures of fantastical creatures such as a diminutive dinosaur and a life-size winged horse, all weathered to the point that they blend into the landscape.

The Rombauer family traces its heritage to another fertile wine area, the Rheingau region in Germany, where Koerner Rombauer's ancestors made wine. His great-aunt Irma Rombauer wrote the classic book *The Joy of Cooking*. The tradition of linking wine to food is carried on today, with every member of the family involved in the daily operation of the winery, from selecting grapes to marketing the final product. K. R. (Koerner Rombauer III) and his sister, Sheana, are now in charge, respectively, of national sales and public relations.

Koerner Rombauer, a former commercial airline captain, and his late wife, Joan, met and married in Southern California, where both had grown up in an agricultural environment. Since they had always wanted their children to have rural childhood experiences similar to their own, they came to the Napa Valley in search of land. In 1972 they bought fifty acres and settled into a home just up the hill from where the winery sits today. Within a few years, they became partners in a nearby winery. Their hands-on involvement in the winery's operations whetted their appetite for a label of their own and for making handcrafted wines with the passion and commitment of the family tradition. Taking advantage of the topography, the Rombauers built their family winery into the side of the hill. Rombauer Vineyards was completed in 1982.

By the early 1990s, the Rombauers realized they had the perfect location for excavating wine storage caves. Completed in 1997, the double-horseshoe-shaped cellar, extends for more than a mile into the hillside. Tours begin in the tasting room, which is personalized with an eclectic assortment of memorabilia from Koerner Rombauer's life. Among the more interesting items are the many signed photographs of famous people as diverse as test pilot Chuck Yeager, entertainer Barbra Streisand, former Secretary of State George Shultz, and country music star Garth Brooks, many of them with personal notes to Rombauer.

ROMBAUER VINEYARDS
3522 Silverado Trail
St. Helena, CA 94574
800-622-2206
707-963-5170
www.rombauer.com

OWNER:
Koerner Rombauer.

LOCATION: 1.5 miles north of Deer Park Rd.

APPELLATION: Napa Valley.

HOURS: 10 A.M.–5 P.M. daily.

TASTINGS: $10, by appointment.

TOURS: By appointment.

THE WINES: Cabernet Sauvignon, Chardonnay, Merlot, Zinfandel.

SPECIALTY: Diamond Selection Cabernet Sauvignon.

WINEMAKER:
Gregory Graham.

ANNUAL PRODUCTION:
50,000 cases.

OF SPECIAL NOTE: Tours include visit to barrel-aging cellar. Copies of the latest edition of *The Joy of Cooking* and other cookbooks by Irma Rombauer are available in the tasting room. Zinfandel Port and Joy, a late-harvest Chardonnay, available only at winery.

NEARBY ATTRACTIONS:
Bothe-Napa State Park (hiking, picnicking, horse-back riding, swimming Memorial Day–Labor Day); Silverado Museum (Robert Louis Stevenson memorabilia); Culinary Institute of America at Greystone (cooking demonstrations).

RUBICON ESTATE

RUBICON ESTATE
1991 St. Helena Hwy.
Rutherford, CA 94573
707-968-1100
800-RUBICON
reservations@rubiconestate.com
www.rubiconestate.com

OWNERS: Francis and Eleanor Coppola.

LOCATION: About 3 miles south of St. Helena.

APPELLATIONS: Rutherford, Napa Valley.

HOURS: 10 A.M.–5 P.M. daily.

TASTINGS: $25 guest fee includes tasting of 5 estate wines.

TOURS: Daily (707-968-1161 for reservations and fees).

THE WINES: Blancaneaux (white blend), Cask Cabernet Sauvignon, Estate Merlot, Pennino Zinfandel, RC Reserve Syrah, Rubicon (red blend).

SPECIALTY: Rubicon.

WINEMAKER: Scott McLeod.

ANNUAL PRODUCTION: Unavailable.

OF SPECIAL NOTE: Historic wine and magic lantern museum. Extensive shop with estate olive oil, books, wine accessories, and gifts. More than 200 acres of organically certified vineyards. Tableside tastings offered at Mammarella's Wine Bar.

NEARBY ATTRACTIONS: Silverado Museum (Robert Louis Stevenson memorabilia); Napa Valley Museum (winemaking displays, art exhibits); Culinary Institute of America at Greystone (cooking demonstrations).

Academy Award–winning filmmaker Francis Ford Coppola and his wife, Eleanor, started making wine at the old Niebaum estate in 1975. Twenty years later, they bought the winery as well as the nineteenth-century château and adjacent vineyards. Flash back to 1879, when Gustave Niebaum, a Finnish sea captain, invested the fortune he acquired in the Alaska fur trade to establish his own winery, Inglenook. He modeled the massive stone château on the estates he had visited in Bordeaux. By the time the Coppolas entered the picture, however, a series of corporate ownerships had left the estate bereft of its reputation, its label, and much of its vineyard land.

The Coppolas reunited the major parcels of the original estate, which they named Niebaum-Coppola, and began restoring and renovating the château and its grounds to their former glory. The European-style front courtyard now graced with grapevines. Nearby, a is illuminated at night. In the vaulted most dramatic creations, a grand imported from Belize. The Coppolas milestones in Inglenook's long,

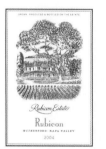

features a redwood and stone pergola ninety-by-thirty-foot reflecting pool entrance is one of Francis Coppola's staircase built of exotic hardwoods also mounted exhibits celebrating illustrious history.

When Francis Coppola set out the acclaimed estate vineyards, he to craft a proprietary red wine using found "the crossing of the Rubicon," Caesar's march on Rome, to be an appropriate metaphor in its implied "point of no return." So it was fitting that he renamed the winery Rubicon Estate in 2006, when the winery introduced profound changes to its image in general and its visitor programs in particular. In the past, thousands of people simply dropped in and wandered around the estate on their own, maybe staying for a tasting or to browse the extraordinary gift shop. To offer a more streamlined, personalized experience, the Coppolas decided to increase the emphasis on wine and education. To that end, visitors are charged a guest fee, good for three days, that entitles them to valet parking, access to the château, and a tasting of five estate wines.

Visitors seeking a more in-depth experience of Rubicon Estate and its winemaking may sign up for any of several educational tours: Sensory, an exploration of the flavors and aromas of selected wines; Elevage, an extensive enological tour covering the various steps in the production of wine and including a visit to the underground caves and a barrel sample; Vinifera, a guided walk in the estate vineyard to learn about the special qualities of the Rutherford appellation; Janus, a food-and-wine pairing with specialties prepared by the executive chef, offered seasonally; and personalized private tours. Most of these tours include wine tasting.

SILVER OAK CELLARS

Fans of fine Cabernet Sauvignon line up hours in advance—sometimes even camping overnight—for the new release of each Silver Oak wine. The vigil has become something of a ritual for connoisseurs who want to be sure to take home some of the winery's hard-to-find bottles. During the early 1990s, on each semiannual release day in Napa Valley, just a handful of people waited for the winery doors to open, but as news of the extraordinary wine spread and the crowds grew larger, Silver Oak Cellars began serving espresso drinks and doughnuts to the early-morning crowds and passing hot hors d'oeuvres throughout the afternoon. Now each release day unfolds at both of the winery's estates, in Napa Valley and Alexander Valley, and many wine lovers plan vacations around the festive events.

The biggest attraction, of course, is what lies in the bottle. Silver Oak produces elegant Cabernet Sauvignons with fully developed flavors and seamless textures. The winemaking program combines meticulous vineyard practices, harmonious blending, and exten- sive aging in exclusively American oak barrels—followed by even more aging in bottles. When the wine reaches the consumer, it is a synergy of depth and delicacy.

The success of Silver Oak Cellars began with two visionary men, Ray Duncan and Justin Meyer. Duncan was an entrepre- neur in Colorado before being lured to California in the 1960s to help a friend work on a vineyard deal. Impressed with the potential for wines in the Napa Valley and the Alexander Valley in Sonoma County, he purchased 750 acres of pastures, orchards, and vineyards within a year. In 1972 he formed a partnership with Meyer, a former Christian Brothers winemaker. The partners' work together lasted thirty years, until Meyer passed away in 2002.

Today the Duncan family sustains the commitment to excellence that has long been a hallmark of Silver Oak Cellars. Each of the two estates is devoted to an individual style of Cabernet Sauvignon. The Alexander Valley wine has a particularly soft and fruity character, while the somewhat bolder Napa Valley wine has firmer tannins, making it appropriate for longer cellar aging. The historic dairy barn that housed the original Napa winery burned in 2006 and was replaced by a new building faced with reclaimed limestone from an abandoned flour mill. The Oakville facility has a hospitality center and tasting room, plus a custom wine cellar that displays Silver Oak's vintages from 1972 to the present. The Alexander Valley winery in Geyserville has an airy tasting room and an inviting courtyard with a fountain for relaxing and enjoying the leisurely pace of Sonoma County.

SILVER OAK CELLARS
Napa Valley:
915 Oakville Cross Rd.
Oakville, CA 94562
Alexander Valley:
24625 Chianti Rd.
Geyserville, CA 95441
800-273-8809
info@silveroak.com
www.silveroak.com

OWNER:
Raymond T. Duncan.

LOCATION: Napa Valley:
1.2 miles east of Hwy 29;
Alexander Valley: 7 miles
from Canyon Rd. exit off
U.S. 101 via Chianti Rd.

APPELLATIONS: Napa Valley,
Alexander Valley.

HOURS: 9 A.M.–4 P.M.
Monday–Saturday.

TASTINGS: $10
(complimentary glass
included). No reservations
required.

TOURS: Monday–Friday,
1:30 P.M.; reservations
recommended.

THE WINE:
Cabernet Sauvignon.

SPECIALTY:
Cabernet Sauvignon.

WINEMAKER:
Daniel Baron.

ANNUAL PRODUCTION:
70,000 cases.

OF SPECIAL NOTE:
Release days are held
simultaneously at both
estates for each wine: Napa
Valley Cabernet on the
first Saturday in February;
Alexander Valley Cabernet
on the first Saturday in
August. Purchase limits on
some vintages.

NEARBY ATTRACTIONS:
Napa Valley Museum
(winemaking displays, art
exhibits).

SILVERADO VINEYARDS

SILVERADO VINEYARDS
6121 Silverado Trail
Napa, CA 94558
707-257-1770
info@silveradovineyards.
com
www.silveradovineyards.
com

OWNERS: Miller family.

LOCATION: About 2 miles
east of Yountville.

APPELLATION: Napa Valley.

HOURS: 10 A.M.–4:30 P.M.
daily.

TASTINGS: $10 for 4 estate
wines; $20 for reserve
wines. Library tasting
with food pairing by
appointment.

TOURS: Of winery and
vineyard by appointment.

THE WINES: Cabernet
Sauvignon, Chardonnay,
Merlot, Sangiovese,
Sauvignon Blanc.

SPECIALTY: Solo Stags Leap
Cabernet Sauvignon.

WINEMAKER:
Jon Emmerich.

ANNUAL PRODUCTION:
Unavailable.

OF SPECIAL NOTE: Limited-
production wines available
only in tasting room.

NEARBY ATTRACTIONS:
Napa Valley Museum
(winemaking displays, art
exhibits); COPIA: The
American Center for Wine,
Food and the Arts.

A steep, curving driveway, worthy of a ski slope, leads to the spectacular site of Silverado Vineyards. On either side of the road, wildflowers cling to the hillsides as if for dear life. Yet nothing compares to the dramatic site of the winery itself, a vision in ocher and terra-cotta, stone and stucco, that brings Tuscany to mind. Many a visitor has noticed that Napa bears more than a passing resemblance to the Italian countryside.

In the mid-1970s, Diane Miller and her husband, Ron Miller, purchased two neighboring vineyards in the Napa Valley. "It was a beautiful land," she says, "and it was a land that was working." For the first few years, the Millers sold their grapes to local vintners, who turned out wines that won gold medals. Inspired by this success, they established Silverado Vineyards in 1981 and then started construction on their own winery, which opened to the public for both tours and tastings in 1987.

2003
CABERNET SAUVIGNON
NAPA VALLEY

Since Silverado was founded, the winery has acquired additional vineyards that it farms itself. Some, notably ninety-five acres of Cabernet Sauvignon and Merlot, are visible from the second-floor tasting room. Guests can sip their wine on a ter-race paved with cobblestones that once graced New York City streets. If you look closely, you can see that some of the stones are worn smooth, while others are set bottom up, with their still-rough surfaces showing. Only a low wall separates the terrace from the abundant vines and wildflowers that bloom throughout the seasons.

The adjacent, spacious tasting room opened in 2000, replacing the much smaller original tasting room in another part of the building. French doors offer north-facing panoramas of vineyards and the hilly Stags Leap landscape. Huge antique beams of Douglas fir, imported from a lumber mill in British Columbia, span the ceiling. Overall, the design is grand but simple, re-calling a Tuscan villa. Across the hall, double doors provide a view of a temperature-controlled barrel cellar. There is no access to the cellar from here, but visitors are invited to open the doors and inhale the heady aroma.

Visitors looking for an intimate Napa wine country experience will want to make reservations for one of Silverado Vineyards' educational tastings and vineyard tours. The library tasting, limited to six participants, features four Cabernet Sauvignons of different vintages, each carefully paired with food. The vineyard tour, also limited to six, offers a walk through the vineyard with a wine educator who talks about how soil and climate influence the wine in your glass. Afterward, guests relax under a 400-year-old oak tree overlooking the vineyard while enjoying Silverado wines and canapés.

SUMMERS ESTATE WINES

Calistoga is about as far away as one could get from the high-pressure, high-density world of high finance. Beth and Jim Summers met in that world, when both were working in San Francisco. Earlier, when he was a commercial lender living in New York, Jim had fallen in love with French wines, especially the reds and particularly anything made with Merlot. Over the years, he had visited the California wine country, and by the time he returned to the West Coast, he vowed never to leave again.

Having grown up in Kansas, Jim Summers figured the best way to stay in Northern California was to buy land, and guided by his financial acumen, he figured the most valuable property would be vineyards in Napa Valley. After some eight years of searching, Summers came upon a wonderful vineyard in Knight's Valley, which is just over the Sonoma County line. In 1987 he purchased the twenty-eight-acre vineyard, which at the time was planted mostly to Merlot and a little Muscat Canelli. Initially, all the grapes were sold to other wineries such as Newton and Ravenswood. The larger than usual harvest of 1992 allowed Summers to produce the first Summers Ranch Merlot—an experience that made him think about all the steps he would have to go through to open his own winery.

After the couple were married, they started looking for a second vineyard. In 1996 they found San Pietra Vara, a winery and tasting room at Highway 128 and Tubbs Lane, about a ten-minute drive from the home ranch. The parcel was an eyesore, but the previous owner had a winery permit and a retail sales permit, so the Summerses decided to buy it. They transformed the weed-infested, junk-strewn site, preserving the existing wonderful "old vine" Charbono and Zinfandel and replanting the remaining acreage to Cabernet Sauvignon. The Napa Valley property is called Summers Estate Wines; the vineyard designation is Villa Andriana Vineyard, named after their daughter. On the remaining two and a half acres, the Summerses installed a hospitality center, a bocce ball court, a picnic area, and a winery and tasting room, which opened in 1997.

The tasting room, which matches the ocher and red color scheme of the adjacent winemaking facility, has an open, refreshing feel, as if it is part of the landscape. Directly across from the entrance is a rectangular tasting bar flanked by French doors that open onto a paved patio with tables and chairs, a fire pit, and a wisteria-covered arbor off to one side. The eye is immediately drawn to the rugged cliffs known as the palisades. Some visitors come specifically to sample the winery's signature Charbono, a little-known Italian varietal rarely grown in California.

SUMMERS ESTATE WINES
1171 Tubbs Lane
Calistoga, CA 94515
707-942-5508
info@summerswinery.com
www.summerswinery.com

OWNERS: Jim and Beth Summers.

LOCATION: About 4 miles north of Calistoga via Hwy. 128 or Silverado Trail.

APPELLATION: Napa Valley.

HOURS: 10:30 A.M.– 4:30 P.M., Monday–Sunday.

TASTINGS: $7 (applicable to wine purchase) for 6 or 7 wines.

TOURS: None.

THE WINES: Cabernet Sauvignon, Charbono, Chardonnay, Checkmate (Bordeaux blend), Merlot, Muscat Canelli, Petite Sirah, Port, Rosé, Zinfandel.

SPECIALTIES: Charbono, Estate vineyards.

WINEMAKER: Ignacio Blancas.

ANNUAL PRODUCTION: 7,000 cases.

OF SPECIAL NOTE: Picnic tables, fire pit, bocce ball court. Winery is kid and dog friendly. Views of Mount St. Helena, Calistoga Palisades, and Old Faithful Geyser. Annual events include Open House Weekend (May). Two-bottle purchase limit on Charbono; Rosé and Muscat Canelli available only in tasting room.

NEARBY ATTRACTIONS: Old Faithful Geyser of California; Robert Louis Stevenson State Park.

SWANSON VINEYARDS

SWANSON VINEYARDS
1271 Manley Ln.
Rutherford, CA 94573
707-967-3500
salon@swansonvineyards.com
www.swansonvineyards.com

OWNER:
W. Clarke Swanson, Jr.

LOCATION: .5 mile west of Hwy. 29.

APPELLATION: Napa Valley.

HOURS: By appointment Wednesday–Sunday, 11 A.M., 1:30 P.M., and 4 P.M.

TASTINGS: Choice of tailored tastings, $30 and $55.

TOURS: None.

THE WINES: Alexis (Cabernet Sauvignon), Chardonnay, Merlot, Petite Sirah, Pinot Grigio, Rosato, Sangiovese, dessert wines.

SPECIALTIES: Alexis, Merlot, Pinot Grigio, small-batch varietals.

WINEMAKER: Chris Phelps.

ANNUAL PRODUCTION: 25,000 cases.

OF SPECIAL NOTE: Tastings include cheese and caviar.

NEARBY ATTRACTIONS: Silverado Museum (Robert Louis Stevenson memorabilia); Napa Valley Museum (winemaking displays, art exhibits).

Time seems to stand still when you step inside the Swanson Salon. Or maybe the salon takes you back to an earlier era of leisure, luxury, and lingering conversation. For forty-five minutes to one hour, guests are guided by the "salonnier" through that day's menu of wines, accompanied by little plates of elegant cheeses and American caviar atop potato chips, and capped with a bonbon made exclusively for Swanson Vineyards.

At the appointed hour, visitors are welcomed by the host into the salon. The fantasy begins when they step into an intimate, intensely decorated room with coral-colored walls adorned by seventeen original paintings, some as tall as eight feet, by noted Bay Area figurative artist Ira Yeager. Together, they make up his *Vintage Peasant* series, most of the works having been created especially for this room. A French stone fireplace, a seventeenth-century Venetian curved-wood portico, and baskets of gnarled Syrah vines create additional visual interest. Then it is time to take a seat at an octagonal table made of Moroccan wood inlaid with agate. A small menu lists the day's offerings, which are already arranged on the table. Beside each place setting, guests also find a fanciful map of the winery and its estate properties, including the Cabernet Sauvignon vineyard in Oakville and the Merlot vineyard in Rutherford.

According to Alexis Swanson, director of marketing, the salon concept coalesced in 2000 as an expression of the Swanson family's affinity for an old-fashioned way of life. "It's all about service and intimacy and obsessive attention to detail," she says. "Every tasting is like a little cocktail party held in each guest's honor. The common thread is a love of wine, but the conversation is never technical. It's all a balance of humor and whimsy, art and theater." One look around the jewel box of a room proves Swanson's point. Details of the decor may change slightly over the years, but the style, established by noted New York interior designer Tom Britt, does not.

Catering to the traveler looking for the less attainable, the salon offers such small-batch wines as Cabernet Sauvignon, Chardonnay, Petite Sirah, and an assortment of dessert wines found only at the Swanson Salon.

TWOMEY CELLARS

One of the very few wineries founded to devote itself to a single wine, Twomey Cellars made its reputation by producing only Merlot. Moreover, all the grapes came from a sole Napa Valley vineyard, the Soda Canyon Ranch. For years, this tight focus has allowed the winemaker to practice painstaking, time-honored techniques that he believes maximize the inherent qualities of the grapes.

Recently, Twomey (pronounced "TOO-mee") Cellars has broadened its focus to include two other varietals, all the while remaining dedicated to making wines that reflect the best of their vineyard and vintage. In 2000 the winery purchased the nine-acre West Pin Vineyard in the Russian River Valley of Sonoma County, an area acclaimed for extraordinary Pinot Noirs. The latest offering is Twomey Sauvignon Blanc, sourced from the winery's Napa Valley estate vineyard in Calistoga.

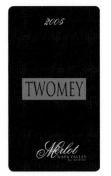

The original Twomey Cellars is located in the northern part of the Napa Valley near the Silverado Trail. The sleek, but intimate tasting room is housed in one of two matching clapboard cottages that stand before the winemaking facility. The gleaming white buildings are surrounded by landscaped gardens and expanses of flourishing vineyards.

In 2007 Twomey Cellars opened a new winery and tasting room on the west side of Healdsburg in the heart of Sonoma's Pinot Noir country. Located only two miles from the West Pin Vineyard, the facility is ideally situated for making handcrafted Pinot Noir. Innovative features such as sophisticated heating and cooling technology permit precise control of temperatures during fermentation and barrel aging, critical functions in producing such a delicate wine. The winery has a striking contemporary design. Glass walls offer expansive views of the landscape, and wraparound patios face Mount St. Helena and Geyser Peak.

Twomey Cellars continues to produce its flagship Merlot at the Calistoga winery. The 145-acre Soda Canyon Ranch in southeastern Napa Valley, the source for the wine, sits on deep volcanic soil and is tightly planted with a particular strain of French Merlot vines selected for their low yield of small, intensely flavored berries. Tempered by cool breezes and morning fog, Merlot ripens slowly and develops rich black-fruit character. Soda Canyon Ranch produces a particularly complex Merlot that warrants meticulous handling by Daniel Baron, one of the few California winemakers versed in *soutirage traditional*, a slow, careful process of decanting the wine from one barrel to another without the disruptive effects of a pump. The procedure, refined over centuries, clarifies red wines to crystal-clear brilliance while drawing the fruit characteristics forward and softening the tannins.

TWOMEY CELLARS
1183 Dunaweal Ln.
Calistoga, CA 94515
3000 Westside Rd.
Healdsburg, CA 95448
800-505-4850
info@twomeycellars.com
www.twomeycellars.com

OWNERS: Duncan family.

LOCATION: Napa Valley, 2 miles south of Calistoga at Hwy. 29; Russian River Valley, Westside Rd. 2 miles from Healdsburg.

APPELLATIONS: Napa Valley, Russian River Valley.

HOURS: 9 A.M.–4 P.M. Monday–Saturday.

TASTINGS: $5 (includes complimentary wineglass).

TOURS: Monday–Friday, reservations recommended. Saturday by appointment.

THE WINES: Merlot, Pinot Noir, Sauvignon Blanc.

SPECIALTY: Merlot.

WINEMAKER: Daniel H. Baron.

ANNUAL PRODUCTION: 10,000 cases.

OF SPECIAL NOTE: Latest vintage of Merlot is released each year on September 1 for limited distribution.

NEARBY ATTRACTIONS: Bothe-Napa State Park (hiking, picnicking, horseback riding, swimming Memorial Day–Labor Day); Robert Louis Stevenson State Park (hiking); hot-air balloon rides; Old Faithful Geyser of California; Petrified Forest; Sharpsteen Museum (exhibits on Walt Disney animator Ben Sharpsteen).

WHITEHALL LANE WINERY

WHITEHALL LANE WINERY
1563 Hwy. 29
St. Helena, CA 94574
800-963-9454
greatwine@whitehalllane.com
www.whitehalllane.com

OWNER: Thomas Leonardini, Sr.

LOCATION: 2 miles south of St. Helena.

APPELLATION: Rutherford.

HOURS: 11 A.M.–5:45 P.M. daily.

TASTINGS: $12 for current releases; price varies for reserve selections.

TOURS: By appointment.

THE WINES: Cabernet Sauvignon, Chardonnay, Merlot, Pinot Noir, Sauvignon Blanc.

SPECIALTIES: Reserve Cabernet Sauvignon, Leonardini Vineyard Cabernet Sauvignon, Rutherford Cabernet Sauvignon, St. Helena Cabernet Sauvignon.

WINEMAKER: Dean Sylvester.

ANNUAL PRODUCTION: 45,000 cases.

OF SPECIAL NOTE: Leonardini family selection wines available only at the winery.

NEARBY ATTRACTIONS: Bothe-Napa State Park (hiking, picnicking, horseback riding, swimming Memorial Day–Labor Day; Culinary Institute of America at Greystone (cooking demonstrations); Silverado Museum (Robert Louis Stevenson memorabilia); Napa Valley Museum (winemaking displays, art exhibits).

Ocher and lavender, the colors of a California sunset, soften the geometric lines of Whitehall Lane, an angular, contemporary structure that stands in contrast to the pastoral vineyard setting. As if to telegraph the business at hand, the building's large windows have been cut in the shape of wine goblets. In front of the winery, a single row of square pillars runs alongside a walkway, each pillar supporting a vine that has entwined itself in the overhanging pergola.

Glass doors open into a tasting room that continues the overall theme with yellow walls, a white beamed ceiling, and a triptych painted with a stylized vineyard scene. The painting befits an estate where the first grapevines were planted in 1880. Even then, Napa Valley settlers were drawn to Rutherford's deep, loamy soils and sunny climate. A vestige of those days, a barn built for equipment storage, is still in use today.

In 1979 two brothers bought the twenty-six-acre vineyard and founded the winery they named after the road that runs along the south border of the property. They produced Merlot and Cabernet Sauvignon before selling the property nine years later. The Leonardini family of San Francisco took over the Whitehall Lane Estate in 1993. Tom Leonardini, already a wine aficionado, had been looking for property to purchase. He was aware of the winery's premium vineyard sources and some of its outstanding wines. Moreover, unlike his previous enterprises, the winery presented an opportunity to create a business that could involve his entire family.

Leonardini immediately updated the winemaking and instituted a new barrel-aging program. He also replanted the estate vineyard in Merlot and Sauvignon Blanc and began acquiring additional grape sources. Whitehall Lane now owns six Napa Valley vineyards, a total of 125 acres on the valley floor: the estate vineyard, the Rutherford West Vineyard, the Bommarito Vineyard, the Leonardini Vineyard, the Fawn Park Vineyard, and the Oak Glen Vineyard. The various wines produced from these vineyards were rated among the top five in the world by *Wine Spectator* magazine.

In 2008 Whitehall Lane completed construction of a new building that contains a barrel room and a crush pad, as well as a second-floor VIP tasting room. The goal of the facility is not to increase overall production, but to focus on small lots of Pinot Noir as well as wines produced from the St. Helena and Rutherford vineyards. Also in the works is the replanting of a portion of the Rutherford West Vineyard with new Cabernet Sauvignon rootstock. As the winery approaches its thirtieth anniversary, the Leonardinis have many reasons to celebrate the success of their family business.

ZD WINES

Driving along the Silverado Trail through the heart of the Napa Valley, travelers are sure to notice the entrance to ZD Wines. A two-ton boulder, extracted from one of ZD's mountain vineyards, is adorned by the winery's striking gold logo, beckoning them to stop for a visit. Calla lilies intertwined with lavender welcome guests as they stroll to the winery entrance. The tasting room provides a cool respite on a hot summer day or a cozy place to linger in front of a fireplace in the winter. Behind the tasting bar are windows that allow visitors to peer into ZD's aging cellars as they sample ZD Chardonnay, Pinot Noir, and Cabernet Sauvignon.

It has been said that winemaking isn't rocket science, but in fact, founding partner Norman deLeuze had been designing liquid rocket engines for Aerojet-General in Sacramento when he met his original partner Gino Zepponi. They decided to collaborate on producing classic Pinot Noir and Chardonnay varietals and needed a name for their new enterprise. The aeronautical industry had a quality-control program with the initials ZD, referring to Zero Defects. This matched the partners' initials and created a new association for the letters ZD. In 1969 the winery purchased Pinot Noir grapes from the Winery Lake Vineyard in Carneros in southern Sonoma and produced its first wine, the first ever labeled with the Carneros appellation. Soon after, the winery started making Chardonnay, which continues to be ZD's flagship wine.

Norman deLeuze turned to winemaking full-time, while his wife, Rosa Lee, handled sales and marketing. They purchased six acres, built their own winery, and planted Cabernet Sauvignon in Rutherford in 1979. Four years later, son Robert deLeuze was named winemaker. He had been working in ZD's cellars since he was twelve and later studied at the University of California at Davis. In 2001 Robert passed the winemaking reins to Chris Pisani, who had worked closely with Robert for five years, building his appreciation and understanding of the family's consistent winemaking style.

As ZD enters its fortieth year of winemaking, it is still owned and operated by Rosa Lee and her three adult children: Robert as wine master and CEO, Brett as president, and Julie as administrative director. Robert's son Brandon began working summers and holidays at ZD in his early teens. Following graduation from Cal Poly San Luis Obispo with an enology degree, he joined ZD as assistant winemaker, bringing the third generation to this family affair.

ZD WINES
8383 Silverado Trail
Napa, CA 94558
800-487-7757
info@zdwines.com
www.zdwines.com

OWNERS: deLeuze family.

LOCATION: About 2.5 miles south of Zinfandel Ln.

APPELLATION: Rutherford.

HOURS: 10 A.M.–4:30 P.M. daily.

TASTINGS: $10 for 3 or 4 current releases; $15 for 2 or 3 reserve or older vintage wines.

TOURS: By appointment. Cellar Tour: $20; Reserve Tour: $30.

THE WINES: Abacus (solera-style blend of ZD Reserve Cabernet Sauvignon), Cabernet Sauvignon, Chardonnay, Pinot Noir.

SPECIALTIES: Cabernet Sauvignon, Chardonnay, Pinot Noir.

WINEMAKERS: Robert deLeuze, wine master; Chris Pisani, winemaker; Brandon deLeuze, assistant winemaker.

ANNUAL PRODUCTION: 30,000 cases.

OF SPECIAL NOTE: Sit-down Vineyard View Tasting on Saturdays and Sundays at 11 A.M. by appointment ($40, 12-person limit) and Monday–Friday by appointment.

NEARBY ATTRACTIONS: Bothe-Napa State Park (hiking, picnicking, horseback riding, swimming Memorial Day–Labor Day); Silverado Museum (Robert Louis Stevenson memorabilia).

SONOMA

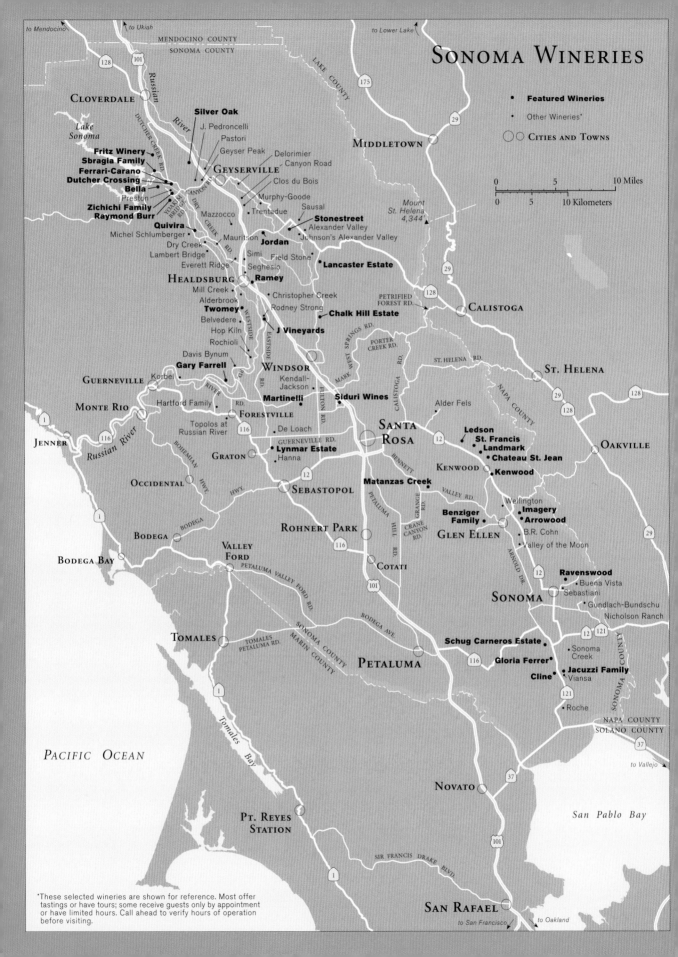

SONOMA WINERIES

• **Featured Wineries**
· Other Wineries*
◯ CITIES AND TOWNS

to Mendocino   to Ukiah   to Lower Lake

MENDOCINO COUNTY
SONOMA COUNTY

LAKE COUNTY

CLOVERDALE

Lake Sonoma

Silver Oak
J. Pedroncelli
Pastori
Fritz Winery
Sbragia Family
Geyser Peak
Delorimier
Canyon Road
Ferrari-Carano
Dutcher Crossing
Clos du Bois
Bella
Preston
Murphy-Goode
Zichichi Family
Raymond Burr
Sausal
Quivira
Trentadue
Mazzocco
Stonestreet
Michel Schlumberger
Mauritson
Jordan
Alexander Valley
Johnson's Alexander Valley
Dry Creek
Simi
Field Stone
Lambert Bridge
Seghesio
Lancaster Estate
Everett Ridge
HEALDSBURG
Ramey
Mill Creek
Alderbrook
Christopher Creek
PETRIFIED
FOREST RD.
Twomey
Rodney Strong
Chalk Hill Estate
Belvedere
Hop Kiln
J Vineyards
Rochioli
Davis Bynum
Gary Farrell
WINDSOR
Korbel
Kendall-Jackson
GUERNEVILLE
Martinelli
Siduri Wines
Alder Fels
MONTE RIO
Hartford Family
FORESTVILLE
Topolos at
Russian River
De Loach
SANTA ROSA
Ledson
St. Francis
JENNER
GUERNEVILLE RD.
Landmark
Lynmar Estate
Chateau St. Jean
Hanna
KENWOOD
Kenwood
GRATON
Wellington
OCCIDENTAL
SEBASTOPOL
Matanzas Creek
Imagery
Arrowood
Benziger
Family
B.R. Cohn
ROHNERT PARK
GLEN ELLEN
Valley of the Moon
BODEGA
COTATI
Ravenswood
Buena Vista
VALLEY
FORD
Sebastiani
BODEGA BAY
SONOMA
Gundlach-Bundschu
Nicholson Ranch
TOMALES
Sonoma Creek
PETALUMA
Schug Carneros Estate
Gloria Ferrer
Viansa
Jacuzzi Family
Cline
Roche
NAPA COUNTY
SOLANO COUNTY

to Vallejo

PACIFIC OCEAN

PT. REYES
STATION

SIR FRANCIS DRAKE BLVD.

NOVATO

San Pablo Bay

MIDDLETOWN

Mount
St. Helena
4,344

CALISTOGA

ST. HELENA

NAPA COUNTY

OAKVILLE

0   5   10 Miles
0   5   10 Kilometers

SAN RAFAEL

to San Francisco   to Oakland

*These selected wineries are shown for reference. Most offer tastings or have tours; some receive guests only by appointment or have limited hours. Call ahead to verify hours of operation before visiting.

Sonoma boasts the greatest geographical diversity in California wine country. From the Pacific Coast to the inland valleys, to the Mayacamas Range that defines the eastern border with Napa County, the countryside is crisscrossed by dozens of rural roads, making it an ideal destination for casual exploration.

Most of the county's oldest wineries can be found in the historic town of Sonoma. Facing the extensively landscaped eight-acre central plaza are nineteenth-century adobe and false-front buildings that now house  upscale shops, restaurants, and inns, as well as historic sites.

In the northern part of the county, the city of Healdsburg has recently evolved from a quiet backwater into the hottest destination in Sonoma County. It sits at the hub of three major grape-growing regions—Russian River Valley, Alexander Valley, and Dry Creek Valley—all within a ten-minute drive of the vibrant town plaza.

North of Santa Rosa, the Russian River Valley extends from the Healdsburg area almost all the way to the ocean, where the Sonoma Coast has become one of the most sought-after wine appellations. In addition to the colorful villages clustered along the coastal routes, the region offers boating, swimming, and fishing opportunities and the shade of giant redwoods that soar above the Russian River's banks.

ARROWOOD VINEYARDS & WINERY

From the highway, the pair of gray, New England farmhouse–style buildings with generous porches neatly trimmed in white could easily pass for a country inn. In fact, the property was originally intended to become a bed-and-breakfast, but it never opened for business. Today, these handsome, sedate structures are home to the Arrowood Vineyards & Winery. The sweeping view from the wide porches encompasses the Arrowood vineyards, a neighboring winery, and the oak-studded slopes of Sonoma Mountain on the western horizon.

Richard Arrowood made his name as the longtime winemaker at Chateau St. Jean, just up the road in Kenwood. A native San Franciscan raised in Santa Rosa, he earned degrees in organic chemistry and enology, and got his start in the business in 1965 at Korbel Champagne Cellars. In 1974 the founders of Chateau St. Jean hired Arrowood as their first employee. For the next sixteen years, he made wines that earned both him and the winery worldwide attention. His reputation as one of the country's best winemakers was firmly established with his late-harvest Riesling, a varietal that he produces today under his own label.

In the late 1980s, he met and married Alis Demers, who had been working in the wine industry since 1978. Together, they began establishing the Arrowood brand. They found the perfect fifteen-acre property and designed their winery to blend harmoniously with the rural landscape. When the couple realized that they had inherited two donkeys, Burt and Ernie, from the previous landowner, they lacked the heart to kick them out and fenced off an area behind the winery.

While Richard was still at Chateau St. Jean, Alis was topping barrels or running the bottling line when she wasn't giving tours and conducting tastings. Richard began working full-time at the winery in 1990, freeing Alis to devote her energies to sales and marketing. Richard began by focusing exclusively on reserve-quality Chardonnay and Cabernet Sauvignon. Before long, he was seduced by the idea of working with less common varietals, particularly when he found exceptional fruit. Today Arrowood produces Malbec, for instance, as well as more familiar wines, all made from Sonoma County grapes.

In 1998 the winery realized a long-cherished dream: opening a spacious Hospitality House next door. The building has a dramatic vaulted ceiling, an enormous stone fireplace flanked by comfortable seating, and a second-floor loft for private events. Picture windows afford magnificent views of Sonoma Valley. Visitors are welcome to walk out the huge glass doors and relax on the wraparound veranda, wineglasses in hand.

ARROWOOD VINEYARDS & WINERY
14347 Hwy. 12
Glen Ellen, CA 95442
707-935-2600
hospitality@
arrowoodvineyards.com
www.arrowoodvineyards.
com

FOUNDERS: Richard and Alis Arrowood.

LOCATION: About 3 miles north of town of Sonoma.

APPELLATION: Sonoma Valley.

HOURS: 10 A.M.–4:30 P.M. daily.

TASTINGS: $5 for 4 wines; $10 for 4 reserve wines.

TOURS: 10:30 A.M. and 2:30 P.M. daily by appointment.

THE WINES: Cabernet Sauvignon, Chardonnay, Gewürztraminer, Malbec, Merlot, Pinot Blanc, red Rhône blend, Riesling (late harvest), Syrah, Viognier, white Rhône blend.

SPECIALTY: All wines are made from Sonoma County grapes.

WINEMAKER: Richard Arrowood.

ANNUAL PRODUCTION: 25,000 cases.

OF SPECIAL NOTE: Extended winery and cellar tours by appointment; events ranging from food-and-wine pairings to educational tastings. Wine accessories, gifts, and apparel sold at winery shop.

NEARBY ATTRACTIONS: Jack London State Historic Park (museum, hiking, horseback riding).

BELLA VINEYARDS AND WINE CAVES

BELLA VINEYARDS AND WINE CAVES
9711 West Dry Creek Rd.
Healdsburg, CA 95448
707-473-9171
866-572-3552
info@bellawinery.com
www.bellawinery.com

OWNERS: Scott and Lynn Adams.

LOCATION: 9 miles northwest of Healdsburg via Dry Creek Rd. and Yoakim Bridge Rd.

APPELLATION: Dry Creek Valley.

HOURS: 11 A.M.–4:30 P.M. daily.

TASTINGS: $5.

TOURS: Group tours by appointment.

THE WINES: Petite Sirah, Syrah, Zinfandel, small lots of Grenache.

SPECIALTIES: Vineyard-designated Syrah, Zinfandel.

WINEMAKER: Joe Healy.

ANNUAL PRODUCTION: 6,500 cases.

OF SPECIAL NOTE: Tasting room is in a 6,700-square-foot cave. Picnic area is partially shaded by 100-year-old olive trees. Limits on the purchase of specialty production wines. Annual events include Winter Wineland (January), Barrel Tasting (March), Passport to Dry Creek Valley (April), Wine & Food Affair (November).

NEARBY ATTRACTIONS: Lake Sonoma (hiking, fishing, boating, camping, swimming).

Located on the banks of Dry Creek, this rustic winery has a fairy-tale quality. The refurbished, red-sided barn, the ancient olive trees with their giant, gnarled trunks, and the vineyards thriving above the cave entrance could be an illustration right out of an old-fashioned children's book.

The tale is a romantic one with a happily-ever-after ending. In 1994 Lynn and Scott Adams came to the Sonoma wine country to get married and fell in love all over again—with the land. They made another vow: to devote themselves to living in a rural setting and to making fine red wine. After all, the Dry Creek Valley has long been famous for its abundance of very old Zinfandel vines known for producing small amounts of  highly flavored grapes. A year later, the young couple bought their first Zinfandel vineyard on ninety-three acres at the western end of the valley. Before long, Lynn and Scott had moved to the area to manage the property. They spent several years taking viticulture classes at the University of California, Davis, and elsewhere before they felt ready to make wine. By the time they opened the winery, they knew exactly what to call the place. Bella is named in honor of their two daughters, who arrived around the same time as their first wine barrels.

To fully realize the rest of their dream—making small lots of fine Zinfandel and Syrah—the Adamses purchased two more low-yielding vineyards not far from their original property. The grapes for Bella's Grenache and estate Zinfandel come from eighty-five-year-old vines at Lily Hill Estate, as the original property is called. Bella also harvests Zinfandel from the Belle Canyon Vineyard on the east side of Dry Creek Valley, where old-clone, low-yielding vines deliver intensely flavored grapes. The third family vineyard, the Big River Ranch on the border of the Russian River and Alexander Valley appellations, is a veritable forest of hundred-year-old Zinfandel, Syrah, and Petite Sirah vines. Bella Vineyards does not need huge crops to make its wines—in fact, quite the opposite. The first vintage, 1999, consisted of only 200 cases. By focusing on single-vineyard wines and limiting production to a maximum of 6,500 cases, the Adamses have the option of postponing release dates until the wine is sufficiently aged and completely ready to drink.

As a family winery located on the quiet backroads of Dry Creek, Bella is appropriately low-key. Tastings are conducted inside the high-ceilinged aging caves, which are furnished with bistro tables and decorated with antique winery artifacts from around the world. The winery and its grounds are a popular destination for those looking for wonderful red wine and who, like Lynn and Scott Adams, find inspiration in the views of vineyards and rolling hills.

BENZIGER FAMILY WINERY

The Benziger family's pride and joy is the snazzy red Massey 375 tractor that takes visitors on forty-five-minute tram tours of the winery's estate vineyards and gardens. Part of the fun is scouting for the songbirds, butterflies, and small animals that populate the estate's three wildlife sanctuaries, along with a host of beneficial insects that provide a natural form of pest control. By encouraging the public to get up close with their eighty-five-acre ranch, the Benzigers share their love of the land and show how they use biodynamic farming practices to cultivate grapes that reflect the specific attributes of each vineyard block.

More than twenty-five years ago, Mike and Mary Benziger drove a short distance up Sonoma Mountain from the hamlet of Glen Ellen. There, abutting author Jack London's historic Beauty Ranch, they found the overgrown property that, with the help of Mike's parents, Bruno and Helen Benziger, would become the Benziger Family  Winery. The couple were soon joined by Mike's six siblings and two dozen members of the clan their parents. Today, more than live on and around the estate.

The Benziger Family Winery formed by volcanic explosions two million years ago that created elevations, and soil profiles. The occupies a 360-degree bowl from Sonoma Mountain some a wide spectrum of sun exposures, Benzigers found that the Sonoma Valley's warm-to-hot days and cool nights are well suited to several grape varieties, particularly Cabernet Sauvignon, which is planted in 65 percent of the estate vineyards.

United not only by blood but also by a commitment to sustainable agriculture, the Benzigers adhere to the highest form of organic farming. Biodynamics requires the elimination of all chemicals and artificial inputs in order to encourage the most natural and healthy environment in and around the vineyards. In 2000 the Benziger property became the first vineyard in either Napa or Sonoma County to be certified biodynamic by the Demeter Association, the only group with that authority. The highest expression of Benziger's winegrowing practices is Tribute, a red Bordeaux blend produced from 100 percent estate grapes that debuted with the 2001 vintage. The winery encourages biodynamic practices among its fifty growers. In all, Benziger has access to some three hundred separate vineyard lots that provide enough variety to warrant bottling more than twenty different wines a year. Visitors do not have to take the tractor-tram tour to sample some of these wines in the tasting room, but it would be a shame to miss the best adventure ride in the wine country.

BENZIGER FAMILY WINERY
1883 London Ranch Rd.
Glen Ellen, CA 95442
888-490-2739
greatwine@benziger.com
www.benziger.com

OWNERS: Benziger family.

LOCATION: About .5 mile from Arnold Dr.

APPELLATION: Sonoma Mountain.

HOURS: 10 A.M.–5 P.M. daily.

TASTINGS: $10 for 5 wines; $15 for 5 reserve wines; $40 for partners tour and tasting.

TOURS: $15 for tram tour and 4 tastings.

THE WINES: Cabernet Sauvignon, Chardonnay, Merlot, Muscat, Petite Sirah, Pinot Noir, Sauvignon Blanc, Syrah.

SPECIALTIES: Bordeaux blends, biodynamic wines.

WINEMAKERS: Mike Benziger, Rodrigo Soto.

ANNUAL PRODUCTION: 185,000 cases.

OF SPECIAL NOTE: Picnic area in redwood grove; children's play area; peacock aviary; display of antique farm and winery equipment; shop with home furnishings and cookbooks. Annual events include Barrel Tasting (March), Pinot Passion (February).

NEARBY ATTRACTIONS: Jack London State Historic Park (museum, hiking, horseback riding); Sonoma Valley Regional Park (hiking, dog park); Morton's Sonoma Springs Resort (swimming, picnicking in summer).

CHALK HILL ESTATE WINERY

CHALK HILL ESTATE WINERY
10300 Chalk Hill Rd.
Healdsburg, CA 95448
800-838-4306
707-657-4837
concierge@chalkhill.com
www.chalkhill.com

OWNERS: Frederick P. Furth and Peggy J. Furth.

LOCATION: About 5 miles from Shiloh Rd. exit off U.S. 101 via Old Redwood Hwy. and Pleasant Ave.

APPELLATIONS: Chalk Hill, Russian River Valley.

HOURS: By appointment, 10 A.M.–4 P.M. daily.

TASTINGS: $10 for 4 wines.

TOURS: Estate Tours ($20, including tasting), Monday–Friday, 10 A.M., 1 P.M., and 3 P.M., by appointment. Culinary Tours ($75, including tour of gardens and vineyards and seated tasting of wines paired with food), Monday and Friday, 2:30 P.M.

THE WINES: Cabernet Sauvignon, Chardonnay, Merlot, Pinot Gris, Sauvignon Blanc, Semillon.

SPECIALTIES: Estate Cabernet Sauvignon, Chardonnay, Merlot, Sauvignon Blanc.

WINEMAKER: Jordan Fiorentini.

ANNUAL PRODUCTION: 30,000–35,000 cases.

OF SPECIAL NOTE: Culinary Tours are conducted in the grand lobby of the equestrian center. Estate Luncheons ($150), by appointment, include tour and four-course meal.

NEARBY ATTRACTIONS: Shiloh Ranch Regional Park (hiking, bicycling).

Few wineries in the United States truly qualify as grand estates, with all that the term implies. The European countryside is dotted with vineyards, villas, and châteaus over a century old, but most American wineries are so new that they appear to have been imposed on the landscape rather than blended into it. The spectacular Chalk Hill Estate is a rare exception and, like many of Europe's most enduring grand estates, not only is esteemed for the quality of its wines but is so multifaceted it could almost be a village unto itself.

Sprawling over 1,477 acres, Chalk Hill provides a microcosm of Sonoma County geography, with heritage oak woodlands,  meandering streams, and high, rolling hills that are often misted with morning fog. The estate's 60 small vineyards are scattered in many different places, creating an intermittent patchwork of seasonal color that ranges from green in late winter and spring to yellow and rust by harvest time in the early fall. Regardless of the time of year, tours of the estate afford an enticing glimpse of Sonoma County's astonishing scenic and geographical diversity. It is a place of peace and plenty that visitors will likely never forget.

From a vineyard manager's point of view, Chalk Hill is not a single estate, but a highly desirable assortment of individual ones. Each plot has been matched with the optimal grape variety for that location and is farmed according to its particular characteristics. In addition to varying topography, there are thirteen different soil types here, part of the geographical complexity of the appellation. An old riverbed caps one hill, for instance, and an unusual serpentine vein ranges through another. Beneath the topsoil lies the distinctive layer of chalk-colored volcanic ash that inspired the name of both the appellation and the estate.

When Frederick Furth first bought property here in 1972, he was determined to live in harmony with the land, rather than to impose himself on it. After Peggy joined him in 1980, the Furths established extensive gardens that provide estate chef Didier Ageorges, formerly with the Ritz-Carlton San Francisco, with fresh organic produce that he selects to go with Chalk Hill wines for food-and-wine pairings as well as other special events.

In addition to the tasting rooms, wines can be sampled along with food pairings by advance reservation. These and other culinary events are held in the grand Pavilion, a conservatory overlooking the equestrian center. In this elegantly furnished, high-ceilinged room, with views of the equestrian center on one side and of the Chalk Hill Valley on the other, guests partake of several small plates prepared by the chef to complement a variety of estate wines.

CHATEAU ST. JEAN WINERY

With the dramatic profile of Sugarloaf Ridge as a backdrop, the exquisitely landscaped grounds at Chateau St. Jean in Kenwood evoke the image of a grand country estate. The château itself dates to the 1920s, but it wasn't until 1973 that a family of Central Valley, California, growers of table grapes founded the winery. They named it after a favorite relative and, with tongue in cheek, placed a statue of "St. Jean" in the garden.

The winery building was constructed from the ground up to suit Chateau St. Jean's particular style of winemaking. The founders believed in the European practice of creating vineyard-designated wines, so they designed the winery  to accommodate numerous lots of grapes, which could be kept separate throughout the winemaking process. Wines from each special vineyard are also bottled and marketed separately, with the vineyard name on the label. The winery produces a dozen vineyard-designated wines from the Sonoma Valley, Alexander Valley, Russian River Valley, and Carneros appellations. The winery also makes other premium varietals and one famously successful blend, the flagship Cinq Cépages Cabernet Sauvignon.

Chateau St. Jean became the first Sonoma winery to be awarded the prestigious Wine of the Year award from *Wine Spectator* magazine for its 1996 Cinq Cépages, a Bordeaux-style blend of five varieties, including Cabernet Sauvignon, Cabernet Franc, and Malbec. The winery received high acclaim again when it was given the #2 Wine of the Year from *Wine Spectator* for its 1999 Cinq Cépages Cabernet Sauvignon. Winemaker Margo Van Staaveren has nearly thirty years of vineyard and winemaking experience with Chateau St. Jean, and her knowledge of Sonoma further underscores her excellence in highlighting the best of each vineyard.

In the summer of 2000, Chateau St. Jean opened the doors to its new Visitor Center and Gardens. A formal Mediterranean-style garden contains roses, herbs, and citrus trees planted in oversized terra-cotta urns arranged to create a number of open-air "rooms." Picnickers have always been welcome to relax on the winery's redwood-studded grounds, but now the setting is enhanced by the extensive plantings, making the one-acre garden attractive throughout the year.

Beyond the Mediterranean garden is the tasting room with a custom-made tasting bar. Fashioned from mahogany with ebony accents, the thirty-five-foot-long bar is topped with sheet zinc. The elegant château houses the Reserve Tasting Room. Visitors who would like to learn more about Chateau St. Jean wines are encouraged to join one of the daily tours of the château and gardens, which include a tasting, or make a reservation for a more in-depth program.

CHATEAU ST. JEAN WINERY
8555 Hwy. 12
Kenwood, CA 95452
707-833-4134
www.chateaustjean.com

LOCATION: 8 miles east of Santa Rosa.

APPELLATION: Sonoma Valley.

HOURS: 10 A.M.–5 P.M. daily, except major holidays.

TASTINGS: $10 in main Tasting Room; $15 in Reserve Tasting Room.

TOURS: History and Vineyard Tour daily at 11 A.M. and 2 P.M. (30 minutes, complimentary).

THE WINES: Cabernet Franc, Cabernet Sauvignon, Chardonnay, Fumé Blanc, Gewürztraminer, Malbec, Merlot, Pinot Blanc, Pinot Noir, Riesling, Syrah, Viognier.

SPECIALTIES: Cinq Cépages Cabernet Sauvignon and vineyard-designated wines.

WINEMAKER: Margo Van Staaveren.

ANNUAL PRODUCTION: 400,000 cases.

OF SPECIAL NOTE: Picnic tables in oak-and-redwood grove. Wine education classes. Open houses on most holidays. Store offering gourmet food and merchandise.

NEARBY ATTRACTIONS: Sugarloaf Ridge State Park (hiking, camping, horseback riding).

CLINE CELLARS

CLINE CELLARS
24737 Arnold Dr.
Sonoma, CA 95476
707-940-4030
www.clinecellars.com

OWNERS: Fred and Nancy Cline.

LOCATION: About 5 miles south of the town of Sonoma.

APPELLATION: Los Carneros.

HOURS: 10 A.M.–6 P.M. daily.

TASTINGS: Complimentary.

TOURS: 11 A.M., 1 P.M., and 3 P.M. daily.

THE WINES: Carignane, Marsanne, Mourvèdre, Pinot Gris, Syrah, Viognier, Zinfandel.

SPECIALTIES: Zinfandel, Rhône-style wines.

WINEMAKER: Charles Tsegeletos.

ANNUAL PRODUCTION: Unavailable.

OF SPECIAL NOTE: Free museum displaying handcrafted models of California's Spanish missions, originally created for the 1939 World's Fair. Aviaries with exotic birds. Cookbooks, deli items, condiments, and gifts sold in winery shop.

NEARBY ATTRACTIONS: Mission San Francisco Solano and other historic buildings in downtown Sonoma; Infineon Raceway (NASCAR and other events); biplane flights; Cornerstone Gardens (innovative designs by landscape architects).

Five thousand rosebushes stand shoulder to shoulder beside the low stone wall that winds its way onto the winery grounds. From April through December, they provide a riot of fragrant pink, white, red, peach, lavender, and yellow blossoms. Picnic tables are scattered around the lawn, shaded by magnolias and other trees. Weeping willows hover over the mineral pools on either side of the restored 1850s farmhouse where the tasting room is located. The white farmhouse is rimmed with a picturesque dark green porch set with small wrought-iron tables and chairs where visitors can sip wine at their leisure.

Cline Cellars was originally established in Oakley, California, some forty miles east of San Francisco. Founder Fred Cline learning farming and winemaking Jacuzzi (of spa and pump fame). with a $12,000 inheritance from the Cline facilities were relocated to appellation at the southern end of

had spent his childhood summers from his grandfather, Valeriano Cline started the winery in 1982 the sale of Jacuzzi Bros. In 1991 this 350-acre estate in the Carneros the Sonoma Valley.

The Cline estate occupies a by the Miwok Indians. Nearby, a to the time when the white settlers had known all along: warm mineral baths are good for you. While the town of Sonoma is generally considered the original site of the Sonoma mission, the mission was actually founded here when Father Altimira installed a cross on July 4, 1823. Perhaps it was the constant Carneros breezes that inspired him to pull up stakes and relocate to the town of Sonoma later that same year.

historical parcel of land first settled nineteenth-century bathhouse harks realized something that the Miwoks

Cline Cellars specializes in Zinfandel and Rhône varietals. The winery's Zinfandel, Ancient Vines Carignane, and Mourvèdre wines are produced from some of the oldest and rarest vines in the state. The Sonoma location was selected especially for its relatively cool climate; chilly fog and frequent strong afternoon winds mitigate the summertime heat that blisters the rest of the Sonoma Valley. When the Clines bought the property, they planted all-new vineyards of Rhône varietals such as Syrah, Viognier, Marsanne, and Roussanne. Since 2000 the winery has practiced a high standard of sustainable and natural farming by following practices that give back to the land and create a self-nourishing ecosystem.

DUTCHER CROSSING WINERY

Dry Creek Valley may boast more family wineries than any other appellation in Northern California. Sixteen miles long and at most two across, the valley has been home to generations of grape growers and winemakers. The laid-back, neighborly ambience still attracts people who love the idea of operating a family business. So it was with Debra Mathy, who shared that dream with her father, a well-respected entrepreneur and family man. A graduate of the University of Arizona with a master's degree in nutrition from Colorado State University, she has been involved in various successful family enterprises over the years.

Together, father and daughter frequently set out from Wisconsin to visit various wine regions throughout California in search of a place to call home where they could establish their own winery. In the spring of 2007, three months after the passing of her father and nearly five years after beginning her search, Mathy finally found her dream location. Here, beside Dry Creek, surrounded on three sides by vineyards, stood a winery that could easily be mistaken for an early 1900s barn, complete with cupolas and a pitched roof. The cedar-plank building is split by a large, open breezeway that serves as a picture frame, affording a view of the panoramic vineyards and hillsides beyond the creek.

The tasting room, located across the breezeway from the production and storage facilities, has wide hickory plank floors, a polished limestone tasting bar, a vaulted beam ceiling, and tall windows on two sides. At one end, a cozy conversational area with comfortable seating faces a fireplace made from locally quarried stone and topped with a mantel fashioned from distressed railroad ties. Throughout the room, works from Mathy's private art collection are displayed on the walls, adding a personal touch to the Americana-style décor. Huge windows behind the tasting bar frame the wooded hills visible on the far side of Dry Creek.

Visitors are often greeted with a special welcome by Dutchess, a golden lab that Mathy adopted from Taiwan and brought home in October of 2007. While Dutchess learned her way around the winery grounds, Mathy picked up some useful words in Taiwanese, such as "sit!" and "let's go!"

Dutchess has plenty of places to romp. The estate vineyard, adjacent to the winery, has rich sandy and silt loam surface soils mixed with some gravel and clay. This profile provides a favorable *terroir* for grapevines, as the roots can extend deeper into the soil. For more than thirty years, this vineyard has been producing outstanding Cabernet Sauvignon grapes. Dutcher Crossing also produces vineyard-designated wines from Dry Creek Valley, Alexander Valley, and Russian River Valley.

DUTCHER CROSSING WINERY
8533 Dry Creek Rd.
Healdsburg, CA 95448
707-431-2700
866-431-2711
info@dutchercrossing
winery.com
www.dutchercrossing
winery.com

OWNER: Debra Mathy.

LOCATION: 6 miles west of the Canyon Rd. exit off U.S. 101, via Canyon Rd. and Dry Creek Rd.

APPELLATION: Dry Creek Valley.

HOURS: 11 A.M.–5 P.M. daily.

TASTINGS: $5 for 4 or 5 wines; $10 for private tasting and tour.

TOURS: ATV vineyard tours by appointment.

THE WINES: Cabernet Sauvignon, Chardonnay, Merlot, Petite Sirah, Port, Sauvignon Blanc, Syrah, Zinfandel.

SPECIALTY: Cabernet Sauvignon blend.

WINEMAKER: Kerry Damsky.

ANNUAL PRODUCTION: 7,000 cases.

OF SPECIAL NOTE: Picnic tables (reservations for parties of six or more); *pétanque* court; limited deli selections available. Select wines available only at tasting room.

NEARBY ATTRACTIONS: Lake Sonoma (swimming, fishing, boating, hiking, camping).

FERRARI-CARANO VINEYARDS & WINERY

**FERRARI-CARANO VINEYARDS
& WINERY**
8761 Dry Creek Rd.
Healdsburg, CA 95448
707-433-6700
customerservice@ferrari-
carano.com
www.ferrari-carano.com

OWNERS: Don and Rhonda
Carano.

LOCATION: 9 miles west
of U.S. 101 via Dry Creek
Rd. exit.

APPELLATION: Dry Creek
Valley.

HOURS: 10 A.M.–5 P.M. daily.

TASTINGS: $5 for 4 classic
wines; $15 for 4 reserve
wines (applicable to
wine purchase). $20–$35
for private tastings,
Monday–Saturday by
appointment.

TOURS: Monday–Saturday
at 10 A.M. by appointment
(800-831-0381).

THE WINES: Cabernet
Sauvignon, Chardonnay,
Late Harvest Black
Muscat, Late Harvest
Semillon, Merlot, Muscat
Canelli, Pinot Grigio,
Pinot Noir, Sangiovese,
Sauvignon Blanc, Syrah,
Zinfandel.

SPECIALTIES: PreVail
(Cabernet Sauvignon),
Siena (Sangiovese blend),
Trésor (Bordeaux-style
blend).

WINEMAKERS: Sarah
Quider, Aaron Piotter.

ANNUAL PRODUCTION:
About 200,000 cases.

OF SPECIAL NOTE: Enoteca
reserve tasting bar open
daily. Tulip hotline:
707-433-5349.

NEARBY ATTRACTIONS:
Lake Sonoma (fishing,
boating, hiking).

Don and Rhonda Carano were introduced to Sonoma County in 1979 while searching for wines to enhance the award-winning wine lists of their hotel, the Eldorado, in Reno, Nevada. The Caranos, both second-generation Italian Americans, were struck by the natural beauty of the area and decided to purchase a seventy-acre parcel in the Alexander Valley that came with a 1904 farmhouse and thirty acres of grapevines.

The acquisition piqued their curiosity about winemaking, and they began taking courses on enology and viticulture at the University of California, Davis. Realizing the potential for the area, the Caranos began to acquire vineyard land in five appellations: Alexander Valley, Russian River Valley, Dry Creek Valley, Anderson Valley, and Carneros. In 1981 the couple founded Ferrari-Carano Vineyards & Winery at the western end of Dry Creek Road in Dry Creek Valley. Six years later, the first wines bearing the Ferrari-Car- ano label, the 1986 Fumé Blanc and the 1985 Alexander Val- ley Chardonnay, were released. Today, Ferrari-Carano produces those wines, as well as a variety of other whites and reds, including such specialties as Siena (a Sangiovese-based blend) and Trésor (a Bordeaux-style blend), and two dessert wines, Eldorado Gold and Eldorado Noir.

In 1997 the Caranos completed Villa Fiore (House of Flowers), the winery's magnificent hospitality center. The 25,000-square-foot Italianate-style building has dramatic stone arches and columns, sienna-colored stucco walls, a tile roof, and limestone accents throughout. Upon entering, visitors find an Italian-Mediterranean décor that includes a honey-colored coffered ceiling of hand-tooled bird's-eye maple and marbleized walls and flooring. A curving stone staircase leads to the barrel cellar where classic columns support a double-vaulted ceiling. A subterranean space, called Enoteca (Italian for "wine library"), has a number of opulent features: a thirty-seven-foot barrel-shaped tasting bar with a black granite top and a dramatic, glass-enclosed wine bottle cellar running the length of the bar. Visitors can make arrangements for a tasting of Ferrari-Carano's limited-production and reserve wines in this elegant space.

The winery is surrounded by five acres of spectacular gardens designed by Rhonda Carano. What began in 1997 as a labor of love took sixteen months just to plan and complete the initial planting. Visitors are invited to stroll the meandering paths and footbridges along a rippling stream captured at both ends by waterfalls that flow into fish ponds. The stunning gardens change color schemes with every season. In the spring, more than 10,000 tulips and daffodils take center stage. Visitors may call the winery for information on the timing of this beautiful display.

FRITZ WINERY

What began as an idyllic family retreat is now a thriving family business on the northern edge of the Dry Creek Valley. Jay and Barbara Fritz were seeking an escape from the summertime fog and urban bustle of San Francisco when they found this rugged, hundred-plus-acre property on a remote hillside back in 1970. They dammed a spring to create "Lake Fritz" and created a home away from home. Son Clayton Fritz spent his childhood summers in this idyllic setting, although he swam in the pond. Now, as in 1979 and as the only one of he is far too busy looking after

it has been a long time since president of the winery built the three siblings to work there, day-to-day operations.

Construction of the winery began when energy crises were commonplace. The idea of creating an energy-efficient, subterranean winery seemed logical, especially given the capacity to construct a gravity-flow production system. The unique three-tier structure allows crushing to be done on top of the winery, and from there the juice is sent underground to the top floor. When the time is ripe, small lots of wine are sent, via one-inch hoses, a level deeper. White wines are aged in a barrel room underground; red wines mature in the adjoining cave. This system eliminates the need for pumping equipment; refrigeration is required only to cool the fermentation tanks.

The family farms Sauvignon Blanc, Zinfandel, and Cabernet Sauvignon vineyards, as well as a choice amount of Malbec and Petite Verdot on the winery's estate in Dry Creek Valley. Increasingly, Fritz buys Pinot Noir and Chardonnay grapes from the nearby Russian River Valley, where the cool climate regulates the ripening of these Burgundian varietals. A portion of the grapes are sourced from Dutton Ranch, known for producing some of the finest fruit in the Russian River area. In the late 1990s, the winery obtained the rights to about twenty acres of Pinot Noir in the Russian River Valley and is now harvesting this beautiful fruit.

Visitors who troop up the hill to the winery can enjoy a view of Lake Fritz from the patio, where market umbrellas provide shade for round tables arranged just outside the tasting room. Rockroses and other hardy plants grow in orderly terraces and give way to wild grasses as the hill slopes down to the water's edge.

FRITZ WINERY
24691 Dutcher Creek Rd.
Cloverdale, CA 95425
707-894-3389
800-418-9463
info@fritzwinery.com
www.fritzwinery.com

PRESIDENT:
Clayton B. Fritz.

LOCATION: About 1 mile southwest of intersection of U.S. 101 and Dutcher Creek Rd.

APPELLATION:
Dry Creek Valley.

HOURS: 10:30 A.M.–4:30 P.M. daily.

TASTINGS: $5.

TOURS: By appointment.

THE WINES: Cabernet Sauvignon, Chardonnay, Estate Zinfandel, Late-Harvest Zinfandel, Pinot Noir, Rosé, Sauvignon Blanc, Syrah.

SPECIALTIES: Cabernet Sauvignon, Chardonnay, Pinot Noir.

ANNUAL PRODUCTION:
18,000 cases.

OF SPECIAL NOTE:
Annual events include Winter Wineland (January), Barrel Tasting (March), Dry Creek Passport Weekend (April). Late-Harvest Zinfandel, Ruxton Chardonnay, and Syrah available only at winery.

NEARBY ATTRACTIONS:
Russian River (swimming, canoeing, kayaking, rafting, fishing); Lake Sonoma (boating, camping, hiking, fishing).

GARY FARRELL WINERY

GARY FARRELL WINERY
10701 Westside Rd.
Healdsburg, CA 95448
707-473-2900
concierge@garyfarrell
wines.com
www.garyfarrellwines.com

FOUNDER: Gary Farrell.

LOCATION: 15 minutes
south of Healdsburg.

APPELLATION: Russian River
Valley.

HOURS: 11 A.M.–4 P.M.
daily.

TASTINGS: $5 for 5 wines;
$10 for 4 reserve wines

TOURS: Daily, by appointment only. Public tours
($15) are at 10 A.M.;
private tours ($25) are at
2 P.M. Both include tastings
paired with artisan cheeses.

THE WINES: Chardonnay,
Pinot Noir, Sauvignon
Blanc, Zinfandel.

SPECIALTIES: Small-lot,
vineyard-designated–
Chardonnay and
Pinot Noir.

WINEMAKER: Susan Reed.

ANNUAL PRODUCTION:
28,000 cases.

OF SPECIAL NOTE: Groups
larger than 10 are
encouraged to make
appointments on weekdays
for touring and tasting.
Tours can be adapted to
accommodate group's
interests and knowledge
level. Each month, artwork
by a local artist is on
display in tasting room.
Most wines are available
only in the tasting room.

NEARBY ATTRACTIONS:
Russian River (rafting,
fishing, swimming,
canoeing, kayaking).

S leepy, winding Westside Road makes for a delightful drive any time of year, but is at its most seductive in springtime, when birds flit through the woods and the warming sun filters through treetops and time seems to come almost to a stop. The northern end of Westside, closer to Healdsburg, is lined with wineries, but down near Wohler Avenue, on the outskirts of leafy Forestville, most structures are likely to be residences. There is little to prepare travelers for the dramatic entrance to Gary Farrell Winery: a sharp turn leads up a driveway so steep that some drivers have to use first gear to  make the ascent. The bicyclists who favor this rarely traveled stretch of Westside either give up and walk their bikes or pedal up, arriving at the tasting room in a state of near exhaustion.

As befits a man who spent two decades working with such viticultural icons as Davis Bynum, Joe Rochioli, and Tom Dehlinger—all of them noted for creating legendary wines from Russian River Valley grapes—Gary Farrell decided to establish his own business in 1982, producing fifty cases of Pinot Noir from the nearby Rochioli and Allen vineyards, two highly regarded estates.

After years of producing his own wines elsewhere (chiefly at Davis Bynum Winery), Farrell opened his eponymous facility in 2000, high on a ridge overlooking a seductive slice of this appellation famed for great Pinot Noirs and Chardonnays. Visitors enter the winery past a grove of ancient redwood trees, and about two steps inside the tasting room, they are likely to simply stop and gape at the sweeping vista of madrones, valley oaks, and redwoods that extends wall to wall behind the tasting bar. The altitude is only four hundred feet, but the steep slopes create the illusion of much greater elevation.

The ambience is woodsy yet pristine: the tasting bar done in cherry wood, beamed ceilings topped with a skylight, minimalist décor. There is little to distract attention from experiencing the wines and focusing on the subtle and not so subtle differences among, say, half-a-dozen Pinot Noirs, each sourced from single vineyards. Most Gary Farrell grapes come from the Russian River Valley, but some are from the Carneros, another appellation acclaimed for both Pinots and Chardonnays.

The tasting experience is always best closer to the source, and recognizing this, the tours include a seated session featuring limited-production wines paired with four specially chosen artisan cheeses from western Sonoma's own Bellwether Farms. In view of the redwoods that define this part of the world, where blankets of fog can often be seen drifting through the trees below and the ridges across the valley, visitors are imbued with a visceral memory of how the Russian River Valley influences the wine in the glass.

GLORIA FERRER CAVES & VINEYARDS

The Carneros appellation, with its continual winds and cool marine air, is known far and wide as an ideal climate for growing Pinot Noir and Chardonnay grapes. The word spread all the way to Spain, where the Ferrer family had been making sparkling wine for more than a century. In 1889 Pedro Ferrer founded Freixenet, now one of the world's two largest producers of sparkling wine.

Members of the family had been looking for vineyard land in the United States off and on for fifty years when José and Gloria Ferrer visited the southern part of the Sonoma Valley. The climate reminded them of their Catalan home in Spain, and in 1982, they acquired a forty-acre pasture and then, four years later, another two hundred acres nearby. They started planting vineyards with Pinot Noir and Chardonnay, the traditional sparkling wine grapes. The winery now cultivates nearly four hundred acres in the Carneros and, in addition to sparkling wines, produces still wines, including Merlot, Pinot Noir, and Chardonnay. The wines have a history of critical success. Within a year of its 1986 debut, the winery won seven gold medals and a Sweepstakes Award at the San Francisco Fair's International Wine Competition.

The winery that José Ferrer built was the first champagne facility in the Carneros. Named for his wife, it was designed after a *masia* (a Catalan farmhouse), complete with terraces, a red tile roof, and thick walls the color of the Spanish plains. Complementing the exterior, the winery's cool interior has dark tile floors and Spanish textiles. The ties to Spain continue in the winery's shop, which offers a selection of cookbooks devoted to Spanish cuisine and the specialties of Catalonia. Also available are several Sonoma-grown products such as Gloria Ferrer's champagne-filled chocolates, mustards and dipping sauces, and a selection of table condiments.

Visitors are welcome to enjoy Gloria Ferrer wines, both still and sparkling, in the spacious tasting room or outside on the Vista Terrace. There they are treated to a breathtaking view of the Carneros and the upper reaches of San Pablo Bay. On a clear day, they can see all the way to the peak of 3,848-foot Mount Diablo in the East Bay. Both still and sparkling wines are aged in the caves tunneled into the hill behind the hospitality center.

Tours of the winery, offered daily, include a visit to these aromatic dark recesses where guides explain the traditional *méthode champenoise* process of creating sparkling wine, during which the wine undergoes its secondary fermentation in the bottle—the one that forms the characteristic bubbles—rather than in the barrel.

GLORIA FERRER CAVES & VINEYARDS
23555 Hwy. 121
Sonoma, CA 95476
707-996-7256
info@gloriaferrer.com
www.gloriaferrer.com

OWNER: Freixenet, S.A.

LOCATION: 4 miles south of town of Sonoma.

APPELLATION: Los Carneros.

HOURS: 10 A.M.–5 P.M. daily.

TASTINGS: $4–10 per glass of sparkling wine; $1–3 for table wine.

TOURS: Daily during hours of operation.

THE WINES: Blanc de Noirs, Brut, Chardonnay, Merlot, Pinot Noir, Syrah.

SPECIALTIES: Brut Rosé, Carneros Cuvée, Gravel Knob Vineyard Pinot Noir, José S. Ferrer Reserve, Royal Cuvée, Rust Rock Terrace Pinot Noir.

WINEMAKER: Bob Iantosca.

ANNUAL PRODUCTION: 150,000 cases.

OF SPECIAL NOTE: Spanish cookbooks and locally made products, as well as deli items, sold at the winery. Annual Catalan Festival (July).

NEARBY ATTRACTIONS: Mission San Francisco Solano and other historic buildings in downtown Sonoma; Infineon Raceway (NASCAR and other events); biplane flights; Cornerstone Festival of Gardens (high-concept landscape installations).

IMAGERY ESTATE WINERY

IMAGERY ESTATE WINERY
14335 Hwy. 12
Glen Ellen, CA 95442
707-935-4515
877-550-4278
info@imagerywinery.com
www.imagerywinery.com

OWNERS: Benziger family.

LOCATION: 3 miles north of the town of Sonoma.

APPELLATION: Sonoma Valley.

HOURS: 10 A.M.–4:30 P.M. daily.

TASTINGS: $10 for 6 wines.

TOURS: None.

THE WINES: Barbera, Cabernet Franc, Cabernet Sauvignon, Lagrein, Malbec, Petite Sirah, Pinot Blanc, Port, Riesling, Sangiovese, Viognier, White Burgundy.

SPECIALTIES: Limited-production varietals.

WINEMAKER: Joe Benziger.

ANNUAL PRODUCTION: 10,000 cases.

OF SPECIAL NOTE: Estate wines available only in tasting room. Gallery of 210 original artworks commissioned by winery; patio seating; picnic area; bocce ball court. Limited-edition wine-label prints and extensive collection of serving pieces at wine shop.

NEARBY ATTRACTIONS: Jack London State Historic Park (museum, hiking, horseback riding); Sonoma Valley Regional Park (hiking, dog park).

Winemaker Joe Benziger brings a connoisseur's mentality to bear in his craft. Rather than taking the customary approach based on well-known varietals sourced from broad appellations, he is more of a risk taker. Producing wines only from uncommon red varietals or single vineyards poses a challenge of his own making, but the reward lies in creating distinctive wines that have earned Imagery Estate a reputation for selectivity and quality.

Imagery Estate Winery's devotion to sustainable organic and biodynamic practices—in the vineyard and in the cellar— is also unconventional but deemed well worth the effort. The Vineyard Collection com- prises select, vineyard-designated wines that showcase the grapes' unique origins (what the French call *terroir*), as expressed through site-specific farming. The Artist Collection focuses solely on limited-availability offerings that highlight the special attributes of both the grape grower and the winemaker—what the winery calls "a coalescence of the arts."

The winery extends this concept a step further by marrying original artworks with the finely crafted wines. Each bottle in the Artist Collection is adorned with a distinctive label produced from original work commissioned from such notable contemporary artists as Robert Arneson, Chester Arnold, Squeak Carnwath, Roy De Forest, Mary Frank, David Nash, Nathan Oliveira, and William Wiley. As a result, the winery is almost as much a gallery as it is a winemaking facility.

The Artist Collection gallery even has its own curator, Bob Nugent, a recognized artist with strong ties to the regional art community. The origin of the Artist Collection dates to 1985, when Joe Benziger happened to meet Bob Nugent at a local polo match. That encounter led to Nugent's creation of a wine label and the commission of works by other artists. Ultimately, Nugent organized the dozens of pieces of original label art into a permanent display in the winery's hospitality center. Like the winemaking facility behind it, the hospitality center is in an off-white modern building that is surprisingly compatible with the bucolic Sonoma Valley.

The most important artist at the winery, however, remains the winemaker. A member of the acclaimed family that runs the nearby Benziger Family Winery, Joe Benziger has been the creative force behind the Imagery wines since their inception. The Imagery Estate wines became so popular that in the summer of 2000 the family moved the entire operation, including the winemaking facili- ties and the artwork, to their property on Highway 12, less than two miles from the Benziger Family Winery. This complex is where visitors now come to taste the wines, enjoy a picnic on the patio, or try their hand at the winery's bocce court, and linger to admire the one-of-a-kind art collection.

J VINEYARDS & WINERY

Judy Jordan founded J Vineyards & Winery in 1986, three years after the Russian River Valley was proclaimed a distinct winegrowing appellation. She was already familiar with the land, the climate, and the grapes—notably Chardonnay and Pinot Noir—for which the appellation is internationally acclaimed. Those are the two primary grapes that go into sparkling wine, which quickly became the winery's major focus.

What began as a small *méthode champenoise* sparkling wine project at her father Tom Jordan's winery on the other side  of Healdsburg has become a model for Russian River Valley sparkling and varietal winemaking. To that end, Judy Jordan hired her longtime friend George Bursick as winemaker in 2006. Bursick, who had spent the past twenty-one years making wines at Ferrari-Carano, immediately took steps to realize Jordan's goal of expanding the winery's portfolio with more *terroir*-driven, small-production bottlings of Pinot Noir, a grape that is famously delicate and prone to sunburn except when grown in areas such as the Russian River Valley, which enjoys the moderating effects of the river itself.

J Vineyards & Winery has long been recognized as a pioneer among American wineries in promoting wine paired with food. Sampling Pinot Noir with licorice-braised Painted Hills beef short rib or Pinot Gris with duck rillettes, quince compote, and Forelle pears creates an indelible memory of how the right combinations bring out the best in both food and wine. Executive chef Mark Caldwell creates a variety of seasonal delights to pair with J's food-friendly varietal and sparkling wines in three different formats that augment the wine-only tastings available in the J Signature Bar.

Judy Jordan continues to evolve the hospitality experience at J Vineyards & Winery. The wine-and-food pairings are now held in three distinct venues designed to enhance the experience, while the tasting room is devoted exclusively to J's Russian River Valley wines.

In the ultra-contemporary tasting room, guests are served at the J Signature Bar that extends across the back of the spacious room. Behind it is an enormous, eye-catching wall in which bubbles appear to be rising. This work of art in jagged glass and fiber optics, as well as the rest of the art in the tasting room, was designed by noted regional artist Gordon Huether. In addition, exquisitely designed wine accessories and stemware from luxury designers, as well as imported serving pieces, fine linens, papers, and gourmet condiments, complement J's commitment to creating the best environment to experience wine with food.

J VINEYARDS & WINERY
11447 Old Redwood Hwy.
Healdsburg, CA 95448
707-431-3646,
800-JWINECO
winefolk@jwine.com
www.jwine.com

OWNER: Judy Jordan.

LOCATION: About 3 miles south of Healdsburg.

APPELLATION: Russian River Valley.

HOURS: 11 A.M.–5 P.M. daily.

TASTINGS: $10 for 4 wines. Reserve tastings with food pairings: Outdoor Terrace, $35, Friday – Monday, 11 A.M.–4 P.M.; Bubble Room, $55, Thursday – Tuesday, 11 A.M.–4 P.M.; Essence, $200 (7 wines paired with a 7-course luncheon plus tour), Thursday, 11 A.M.–3 P.M.

TOURS: 11 A.M. and 2:30 P.M. daily, by appointment.

THE WINES: Brut and Rosé sparkling wines, Chardonnay, Pinotage, Pinot Noir, Ratafia (dessert wine), Vin Gris, Viognier, Zinfandel.

SPECIALTIES: Cool-climate, site-specific Russian River Valley Pinot Noir and Chardonnay; *méthode champenoise* sparkling wines.

WINEMAKER: George Bursick.

ANNUAL PRODUCTION: 60,000 cases.

OF SPECIAL NOTE: Annual events include Varietal Release (May).

NEARBY ATTRACTIONS: Russian River (swimming, canoeing, kayaking, rafting, fishing).

JACUZZI FAMILY VINEYARDS

JACUZZI FAMILY VINEYARDS
24724 Arnold Dr.
Sonoma, CA 95476
707-931-7575
www.jacuzziwines.com

OWNERS: Fred and Nancy Cline.

LOCATION: About 5 miles south of the town of Sonoma.

APPELLATION: Los Carneros.

HOURS: 10 A.M.–5:30 P.M. daily.

TASTINGS: Complimentary.

TOURS: Available upon request ($15–$25).

THE WINES: Aleatico, Arneis, Barbera, Cabernet Sauvignon, Chardonnay, Dolcetto, Giuseppina, Lagrein, Merlot, Muscato, Nebbiolo, Nero d'Avola, Pinot Grigio, Pinot Noir, Primitivo, Sangiovese, Valeriano.

SPECIALTIES: Italian varietals.

WINEMAKER: Charlie Tsegeletos.

ANNUAL PRODUCTION: Unavailable.

OF SPECIAL NOTE: Most wines sold only at winery. Courtyard tables with market umbrellas for picnics. Cookbooks, specialty foods, home décor items, and gifts sold in winery shop. The Olive Press, producer of oil from local olives, is on-site.

NEARBY ATTRACTIONS: Mission San Francisco Solano in downtown Sonoma; Schellville Airport (biplane rides); Cornerstone Gardens (innovative designs by landscape architects).

The winery's rustic stone-and-plaster exterior offers visitors their first hint of the Jacuzzi family's long, rich history, which reaches back to the Friuli region of northeastern Italy. The unmatched facades on either side of the entry are intentional: the building was designed after the family's ancestral home, created over time by various artisans using slightly different stones. Although the 18,000-square-foot winery was completed in 2007, the use of traditional architectural detailing, natural materials, and a variety of roof forms purposefully creates the impression that it was built centuries ago.

The complex of similar, small structures is organized around a central courtyard that provides the inviting ambience associated with the sharing of food, wine, and hospitality. The winery, like many of the wines themselves, pays homage to the Jacuzzi family's parents, two siblings among seven brothers and six sisters who arrived in the United States in the early twentieth century and went on to achieve great success in their new country.

Inside the stately entrance, monastery-like white walls soar to rustic beamed ceilings in the spacious hall. To the left is the tasting room, which has a bar made from downed oak and walnut trees in the Sonoma Valley. The slats of wood below the surface of the tasting bar have been fashioned to look like the curved staves of wine barrels. True to the family's commitment to hospitality, tastings of the winery's many Italian varietal wines are complimentary.

Wide hallways lead to an interior courtyard typical of vernacular Friuli architecture. Here, several tables graced with market umbrellas offer expansive views of the vineyards. The courtyard faces a spectacular marble fountain, where a larger-than-life figure of Neptune arises triumphantly among gigantic, water-spouting horses.

Nearby, stairs climb to a viewing area overlooking the wetlands of San Pablo Bay as well as distant mountain ranges. The second floor is also home to an informal family museum where photographs and other memorabilia commemorate the Jacuzzi legacy of innovation. One of the earliest inventions was the so-called toothpick propeller, made of laminated wood and utilized on World War I airplanes. Fred Cline, the founder of both Jacuzzi Family Vineyards and Cline Cellars across the road, is the maternal grandson of Valeriano Jacuzzi, one of the seven brothers who participated in the creation of the Jacuzzi spa. What turned out to be a revolutionary concept started in 1948 when the brothers figured out how to treat a family member's arthritis symptoms with a hydrotherapy pump, leading to the family's most famous invention and the launching of a major industry.

JORDAN VINEYARD & WINERY

Parts of Sonoma County resemble the French wine country, but mostly in a topographical sense. The picture always lacked a key element: a grand château. That changed in 1972, when Tom Jordan established his 1,500-acre estate on an oak-studded knoll in the Alexander Valley. Inspired by several eighteenth-century châteaus in southwestern France, the winery was designed by the San Francisco architectural firm of Backen, Arrigoni & Ross. The building, with its wine-red doors and shutters, also serves as a visual metaphor for the winemaking philosophy at Jordan, where Cabernet Sauvignon is blended in the Bordeaux style and Chardonnay is crafted in the time-honored tradition of a white Burgundy.

As visitors approach on the winding driveway, they are teased with glimpses of the château until they reach the top of the hill and can see the entire structure and its landscaped grounds. The image of an old-world estate is furthered by the formal French gardens with their clipped privet hedges, poplar trees, and pollarded sycamores. Boston ivy clinging to the château walls changes colors with the seasons. Gracing the entrance is a small bronze statue of Bacchus, a copy of Jacopo Sansovino Tatti's 1512 original in the National Museum in Florence. From the hilltop, every vantage affords panoramic vistas of the Alexander Valley and its most dramatic focal points, Geyser Peak and Mount St. Helena. It was ancient volcanic activity from Geyser Peak, along with eons of seismic uplift, that formed the narrow, twenty-mile-long valley named for the pioneering family who began farming this area in 1847.

The land Tom Jordan acquired in 1972 included 275 acres for vineyards and another 1,300 acres of rolling oak woodlands, plus two lakes. There would be plenty of room for a winery facility as well as an informal preserve for wildlife. In 1995 Jordan began planting a grove of Tuscan olive trees that now produce fruit for the winery's award-winning organic extra-virgin olive oil.

Jordan's well-educated and enthusiastic personnel take guests on a comprehensive journey from the early years to the Jordan Winery of today. Winemaking is covered in some detail in the production facility. Each tour culminates with a tasting of current releases and a selection of artisan cheeses in the comfortable cellar room, where guests are invited to linger.

JORDAN VINEYARD & WINERY
1474 Alexander Valley Rd.
Healdsburg, CA 95448
707-431-5250
800-654-1213
info@jordanwinery.com
www.jordanwinery.com

OWNER: Thomas Jordan.

LOCATION: About 4 miles northeast of Healdsburg via Hwy. 128.

APPELLATION: Alexander Valley.

HOURS: 8 A.M.–5 P.M. Monday–Friday; 9 A.M.– 4 P.M. Saturday. Open Sundays May–October.

TASTINGS: By appointment.

TOURS: By appointment.

THE WINES: Cabernet Sauvignon, Chardonnay.

SPECIALTIES: Alexander Valley Cabernet Sauvignon, Russian River Chardonnay.

WINEMAKER: Rob Davis.

ANNUAL PRODUCTION: 90,000 cases.

OF SPECIAL NOTE: Extensive landscaped grounds and gardens, including Tuscan olive trees. Jordan olive oil sold at winery. Library, dessert, and large-format wines available only at winery.

NEARBY ATTRACTIONS: Lake Sonoma (boating, camping, hiking, fishing, swimming); Jimtown Store (country market, homemade foods).

KENWOOD VINEYARDS

KENWOOD VINEYARDS
9592 Hwy. 12
Kenwood, CA 95452
707-833-5891
info@heckestates.com
www.kenwoodvineyards.com

OWNER: F. Korbel & Bros.

LOCATION: 15 miles southeast of Santa Rosa.

APPELLATION: Sonoma Valley.

HOURS: 10 A.M.–4:30 P.M. daily.

TASTINGS: Complimentary; $5 for Private Reserve wines.

TOURS: None.

THE WINES: Cabernet Sauvignon, Chardonnay, Gewürztraminer, Merlot, Pinot Noir, Sauvignon Blanc, sparkling wines, White Zinfandel, Zinfandel.

SPECIALTIES: Artist Series, Jack London Ranch wines.

WINEMAKER: Pat Henderson.

ANNUAL PRODUCTION: 550,000 cases.

OF SPECIAL NOTE: Monthly themed food-and-wine events matching chef's specialties with appropriate wines. Limited-release Artist Series wines available only at winery.

NEARBY ATTRACTIONS: Jack London State Historic Park (museum, hiking, horseback riding); Sugarloaf Ridge State Park (hiking, camping, horseback riding).

The photogenic, century-old barn where visitors come to taste Kenwood's wines dates to one of the most romantic eras in Sonoma Valley history. The quintessential adventure author Jack London was living, writing, and raising grapes in nearby Glen Ellen when the Pagani Brothers established their winery in 1906 in the buildings that now house Kenwood Vineyards. In those days, long before the invention of tasting rooms, wine lovers would bring their own barrels and jugs to be filled and then cart them home.

Decades later, in 1970, a trio of wine enthusiasts from the San Francisco Bay Area founded Kenwood Vineyards. In redesigning and modernizing the existing winery, they created a facility that allows the winemaker the utmost in flexibility. More than 125 stainless steel ferment- ing and upright oak tanks are utilized in combination with some seventeen thousand French and American oak barrels. Kenwood uses estate fruit as well as grapes from some of Sonoma County's best vineyards and follows the cuvée winemaking method, in which the harvest from each vineyard is handled separately to preserve its individual character. According to Michael Lee, one of the winery's founders and who is also a wine- maker, such "small lot" winemaking allows each lot of grapes to be brought to its fullest potential before blending. Likewise, the acclaimed Artist Series is a masterful blend of the top barrels of Cabernet Sauvignon.

The historic barn and other original buildings lend a nostalgic ambience to the modern wine-making facilities on the twenty-two-acre estate. But there is another link to the romantic history of the Valley of the Moon, as author London dubbed Sonoma Valley.

Best known for his rugged individualism and dynamic writing, London was also an accomplished farmer and rancher. At the heart of his Beauty Ranch—now part of the Jack London State Historic Park—several hundred acres of vineyards were planted in the 1870s on terraced slopes. The volcanic ash fields produced excellent wines by the turn of the twentieth century. London died in 1916, and by World War II, his crop fields had become overgrown. But in 1976, Kenwood Vineyards became the exclusive marketer of wines produced from the ranch. The Cabernet Sauvignon, Zinfandel, Merlot, and Pinot Noir, made only from Jack London vineyard grapes, bear a label with the image of a wolf's head, London's signature stamp.

Known for consistency of quality in both its red and its white wines, Kenwood produces mostly moderately priced wines. The major exception is the Artist Series Cabernet Sauvignons, which have been collector's items since first released in 1978.

LANCASTER ESTATE

A small, family-owned winery, Lancaster Estate was founded in 1995 with the goal of producing only the finest estate-grown Cabernet-based wines. Located beside the narrow and less-traveled roads of southern Alexander Valley, the winery evokes the rich agricultural heritage of this acclaimed appellation.

This winery off the beaten path in the foothills of the western Mayacamas Range was singled out by *Food and Wine Magazine* as one of the top ten wineries to visit in Sonoma County. Blessed

with a favorable growing climate consisting of warm days and cool nights, the estate also benefits from a complex of volcanic soil types—ideal for growing Cabernets of distinction. Lancaster Estate consists of seventy-two acres in total, with fifty-three acres planted exclusively to the classic Bordeaux varietals—Cabernet Sauvignon, Cabernet Franc Merlot, Malbec, and Petit Verdot.

Visitors enter the estate driveway from twisting, two-lane Chalk Hill Road and are immediately treated to views of gently rolling hillside vineyards and majestic oaks. Guests, who are welcome by appointment only, get a close look at the property, from grapevines to wine tasting, during their approximately ninety-minute visit. First, they are chauffeured—in groups of up to four—around the vineyards in the estate SUV. Then they are escorted to the winery's nine-thousand-square-foot underground cave, where Lancaster Estate ages its wines for twenty-two months in French oak barrels in a naturally controlled setting that maintains the perfect temperature and humidity conditions. Here, guests learn about the estate's growing practices, its production techniques, and its philosophy of aging wines as gently as possible.

A niche has been carved out of the cave's southern wall to create an intimate library, a dramatically decorated room where halogen lights beam down on a tall circular table. More than seven hundred bottles of wine, representing every vintage since 1996, are stored along one wall within arm's reach. Although the library is reserved for VIP tastings, visitors are welcome to take a peek—and even a photograph or two.

The tour, which is complimentary for up to six people, concludes with a tasting of three current-release wines in an elegant, cool cave setting carved within "No Name Hill." Upon entering, visitors travel through a softly lit passage before arriving for their tasting.

LANCASTER ESTATE
15001 Chalk Hill Rd.
Healdsburg, CA 95448
707-433-8178
hospitality@lancaster-estate.com
www.lancaster-estate.com

OWNERS: Ted and Nicole Simpkins.

LOCATION: Less than 11 miles east of Healdsburg via Alexander Valley Rd.

APPELLATION: Alexander Valley.

HOURS: 10 A.M.–4 P.M. Monday–Saturday.

TASTINGS: By appointment. Complimentary for up to 6 people. $15 per person thereafter. Features 3 current-release wines.

TOURS: By appointment. Complimentary vineyard and winery tour for up to 6 people. $15 per person thereafter.

THE WINE: Cabernet Sauvignon.

SPECIALTY: Cabernet Sauvignon.

WINEMAKER: Jennifer Higgins.

ANNUAL PRODUCTION: 4,250 cases.

OF SPECIAL NOTE: Annual events available by invitation only. Lancaster Estate Nicole's Proprietary Red Wine (250 cases produced) and other limited-release wines available only at the winery.

NEARBY ATTRACTIONS: Lake Sonoma (boating, camping, hiking, fishing, swimming); Jimtown Store (country market, homemade foods).

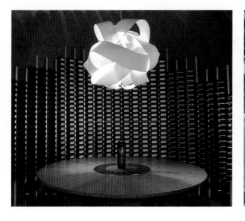

LANDMARK VINEYARDS

LANDMARK VINEYARDS
101 Adobe Canyon Rd.
Kenwood, CA 95452
707-833-0218
info@landmarkwine.com
www.landmarkwine.com

OWNERS: Mike and Mary Colhoun.

LOCATION: Intersection of Hwy. 12 and Adobe Canyon Rd., approximately midway between Sonoma and Santa Rosa.

APPELLATION: Sonoma Valley.

HOURS: 10 A.M.–4:30 P.M. daily.

TASTINGS: $5 for 3 wines; $10 for 3 reserve wines; $15 for special flight.

TOURS: Vineyard tour and tasting 11 A.M., by appointment ($15).

THE WINES: Chardonnay, Pinot Noir, Syrah.

SPECIALTIES: Chardonnay and single-vineyard wines.

WINEMAKER: Eric Stern.

ANNUAL PRODUCTION: 28,000 cases.

OF SPECIAL NOTE: Guest cottage and suite available for overnight stays. Horse-drawn wagon rides through vineyards on Saturdays in summer. Picnic fare and seating available. Single-vineyard wines available only in tasting room.

NEARBY ATTRACTIONS: Sugarloaf Ridge State Park (hiking, camping, horseback riding), Annadel State Park (hiking, biking).

This tidy, twenty-acre estate at the foot of Sugarloaf Mountain represents a melding of the owners' agricultural heritage, the winery's historical architectural style, and a reverence for wine as an integral component of social interaction. At its center is a five-thousand-square-foot courtyard where visitors may mingle, enjoy wines with delicacies from the tasting room, and take in the impressive view of the forested mountain slopes that tower over the town of Kenwood.

Although the winery made its mark initially with two notable Burgundian grapes, Chardonnay and Pinot Noir, it has continued the innovative agricultural traditions of its founding family by adding Rhône varieties such as Syrah, Grenache, Mourvèdre, Syrah, and Counoise, a lesser-known red grape selected for blending purposes. Wine aficionados who are unable to grow their own grapes can adopt a row of grapevines at Landmark, entitling them to have their name on a plaque in the new vineyards closest to the winery.

Landmark Vineyards was established in 1974 by Damaris Deere Ford. A great-great-granddaughter of John Deere, whose 1838 invention of the steel plow revolutionized the business of agriculture, she had the Spanish mission-style winery built in 1989. With the help of renowned landscape architect Morgan Wheelock, the winery grounds were developed into a lush estate embellished with poplar trees, rosebushes, and flowering vines suspended from the eaves. A tall, graceful fountain is the visual centerpiece of the courtyard.

Michael Deere Colhoun and his wife, Mary Colhoun, continue to expand aspects of the winery's hospitality. Beyond the courtyard, visitors will find an area for lawn games and picnic tables in the shade of a century-old walnut tree. All this and much more can be seen from the President's Tower above the tasting room, the location of private, catered events.

Another view of the property has been captured on canvas by Sonoma County artist Claudia Wagar. Her dramatic mural behind the granite bar in the tasting room is a fanciful rendering of the view from one of Landmark's estate vineyards, progressing from a close-up of a grape cluster to Sugarloaf Mountain in the background. In the tasting room, visitors sample wines from the estate vineyards as well as from a range of other vineyards selected as the finest representatives of California's diverse microclimates. True to the proprietors' focus on family, the wine labels reflect their John Deere heritage: Landmark and Overlook Chardonnays were named for family homes, Grand Detour Pinot Noir recalls the location of the Deeres' original blacksmithing shop in Illinois, and Steel Plow Syrah is aptly named for the invention that made it all possible.

LEDSON WINERY & VINEYARDS

It came to be known widely as "the castle"—some people say it reminds them of a French Castle in Normandy. The architectural showpiece took ten years and some two million bricks to build. When the Ledson family started construction in 1992, they thought the property would be ideal for their residence. They planted Merlot vineyards and began work on the house. As the months passed, the turrets, slate roofs, balconies, and fountains took shape, and passersby would even climb over the fence to get a better look.

Steve Ledson finally realized it was time to rethink his plan. Given the intense public interest in the building and the quality of the grape harvests—which were sold to nearby wineries—he decided to turn the sixteen-thousand-square-foot structure into a winery and tasting room. In 1997 he released the winery's first wine: the 1994 Estate Merlot. After two years of reconstruction, the winery opened in 1999.

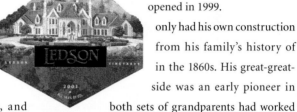

Fortunately, Ledson not only had his own construction company but also benefited from his family's history of farming in the area, beginning in the 1860s. His great-great-grandfather on his mother's side was an early pioneer in Sonoma County winemaking, and both sets of grandparents had worked adjoining Sonoma Valley ranches cooperatively. Eventually, this Ledson acreage became part of the Annadel State Park. The family had grown grapes for years, so Steve, the fifth generation to farm in the area, jumped at the chance to buy the twenty-one-acre property to plant Estate Merlot. The property just happened to have a view of Annadel State Park.

Visitors to the castle find an estate worthy of the French countryside, with a grand brick driveway, a manicured landscape, and a flourishing collection of roses. Just inside the front door is a grand staircase that reminds people of the movie *Gone with the Wind*. The castle has more than five miles of ceiling moldings and sixteen thousand square feet of hardwood flooring spread over four floors of twenty-seven rooms, each with a different pattern of wood inlays. Twelve rooms are visible to the public: nine tasting rooms, a gourmet marketplace, a parlor area, and a club room.

At Ledson, visitors are treated to a sensory feast. The Gourmet Marketplace features a tempting selection of gourmet meats, artisan cheeses, fresh made-to-order sandwiches, salads, and desserts, as well as an extensive selection of locally produced gourmet items. Guests can enjoy a picnic lunch outdoors at tables overlooking the estate vineyards and fountains, or in the castle's intimate parlor with its elegant Italian marble fireplaces and breathtaking views.

LEDSON WINERY & VINEYARDS
7335 Hwy. 12
Kenwood, CA 95409
707-537-3810
www.ledson.com

OWNER: Steve Noble Ledson.

LOCATION: About 2 miles northwest of Kenwood.

APPELLATION: Sonoma Valley.

HOURS: 10 P.M.–5 P.M. daily

TASTINGS: $5–$15 for 5 wines; $25 for private tasting of wines and gourmet cheeses.

TOURS: Self-guided.

THE WINES: Barbera, Cabernet Franc, Cabernet Sauvignon, Carignane, Chardonnay, Grenache, Malbec, Merlot, Meritage, Mourvèdre, Orange Muscat, Petite Sirah, Petit Verdot, Pinot Noir, Port, Riesling, Sangiovese, Sauvignon Blanc, Syrah, Zinfandel.

SPECIALITIES: Small lots of handcrafted Cabernet Sauvignon, Chardonnay, Merlot, Sauvignon Blanc, Zinfandel.

WINEMAKER: Steve Noble Ledson.

ANNUAL PRODUCTION: 35,000 cases.

OF SPECIAL NOTE: Wines available only at winery, hotel, and online. Market offering gourmet foods. Six-room Ledson Hotel & Harmony Lounge, in Sonoma on Sonoma Plaza, includes wine bar.

NEARBY ATTRACTIONS: Annadel State Park (hiking, biking).

LYNMAR ESTATE

LYNMAR ESTATE
3909 Frei Rd.
Sebastopol, CA 95472
707-829-3374
info@lynmarestate.com
www.lynmarestate.com

OWNER: Lynn Fritz.

LOCATION: About 5 miles west of U.S. 101 via Guerneville Rd.

APPELLATION: Russian River Valley.

HOURS: 10 A.M.–5 P.M. daily.

TASTINGS: $10 for 4 or 5 wines; $25 for 4 or 5 reserve wines.

TOURS: By appointment, Friday, 10:30 A.M.–1 P.M.

THE WINES: Chardonnay, Pinot Noir, Syrah, Viognier.

SPECIALTY: Pinot Noir.

WINEMAKER: Hugh Chappelle.

ANNUAL PRODUCTION: 12,000 cases.

OF SPECIAL NOTE: Food-and-wine pairings available Friday–Sunday at 1:30 P.M. ($45 by advance reservation). Pizza and Pinot Fridays during summer 4:30–6:30 P.M. ($35–$45, depending on wine selection). Estate tour takes visitors to wine caves. Annual events include Harvest Celebration (October).

NEARBY ATTRACTIONS: Laguna de Santa Rosa (freshwater wetlands with wildlife viewing).

Once visitors to Lynmar Estate are greeted, comfortably seated, and then served a flight of wines in the appropriate Riedel glassware, they may very well be inclined to stay right where they are for the remainder of the day. The best seats are not in the winery's hospitality salon but on a terrace overlooking the vineyards as well as Laguna de Santa Rosa, a 250-square-mile watershed that is a haven for mammals, reptiles, migrating birds, and native plants. This is one of the most idyllic settings in the entire Russian River Valley.

Lynmar Estate is owned by Lynn Fritz, former CEO of Fritz Companies and currently the head of his humanitarian nonprofit, the Fritz Institute. Fritz bought the forty-eight-acre Quail Hill Ranch in 1980 and began meticulously planting grapes long before the winery was built on the property, which is flanked by highly regarded vineyards owned by Merry Edwards, Kistler Vineyards, and Paul Hobbs. For the first few years, Fritz sold his grapes to other producers before deciding that the quality of the fruit was so outstanding that he should make the wine himself. Lynmar was founded in 1990 and produced its inaugural 1994 vintage of Pinot Noirs and Chardonnays in 1996.

Designed by San Francisco's Baum Thornley Architects, Lynmar's hospitality salon opened in late 2005 as one of a new generation of destination wineries. It is built of wood and stone with a board-and-batten finish, and is reminiscent of a fine, elegant residence rather than a commercial enterprise. The all-wood interior and glass-walled wine library provide a soothing environment for visitors who prefer tasting wine indoors. Set amid vineyards, both the tasting room and the nearby state-of-the-art gravity-flow winery with small stainless steel fermentors and magnificent caves were intended to blend into the surrounding landscape rather than to distract from the natural beauty of the lush Russian River Valley.

Lynmar's estate Quail Hill Vineyard lies within one of the appellation's coolest areas, Laguna Ridge, an enviable microclimate for its primary grape varieties, Pinot Noir and Chardonnay. As evidence of Lynmar's environmental awareness and sensitivity to the stewardship of the land, the winery employs sustainable farming techniques that are gentle on the region's natural resources. Adjacent to the courtyard are organic gardens filled with both edible and purely ornamental plants. Some of the former find their way onto the small plates created by the winery's in-house chef. The menus change seasonally: Pinot Noir paired with a ramekin of butternut squash, pancetta, and mushroom risotto is sufficient for a wintertime lunch, for example, and a Chardonnay might be matched with savory shortbread, aged Gouda cheese, and an onion relish.

MARTINELLI WINERY

The bright red hop barn sitting only a few yards off River Road is a photo opportunity waiting to happen. The tasting room entrance is a sheltered nook where wooden tables and benches, gracefully weathered to a soft gray, sit beneath a vine-covered trellis. Beyond the barn, rows of vineyards march up a hill, interspersed with a trio of arbors perfect for picnicking.

The scene could well be the setting for an old-fashioned movie romanticizing rural life, but the Martinelli Winery is the real thing. The Martinelli family has been growing grapes in the Russian River Valley since 1887, and successive generations have kept their immigrant ancestors' dreams alive over the decades.

At the tender ages of nineteen and sixteen, Giuseppe Martinelli and Luisa Vellutini eloped from their village in the  Tuscany region of Italy, bound for California in search of land where they could start a winery. Giuseppe had been a winemaker in Italy, and with his knowledge of viticulture, he was hired by a local farmer to work in a vineyard in Forestville. Within two years, the hardworking young man was able to purchase some land. Giuseppe and Luisa, working side by side on a sixty-degree slope, planted Zinfandel and Muscat Alexandria vines on what would eventually become known as the Jackass Hill vineyard. Luisa's uphill struggle was just beginning. Giuseppe died in 1918, leaving his widow with four children and a farm to run. The youngest Martinelli son, Leno, left school after the eighth grade and began farming the Zinfandel vineyard all by himself. How did the vineyard get its name? Leno's family told him that only a jackass would farm a hill that steep.

Armed with his parents' knowledge and his own experience, Leno persevered, even using a horse and plow to work the land until 1949, when he finally bought a tractor. Only at the age of eighty-nine did he finally hang up the keys to his John Deere and relinquish the reins to his son, Lee. In 1973 Lee took over management of his uncle Tony Bondi's adjacent estate, located just below Jackass Hill, and planted vineyards where apple orchards once flourished.

When Lee and his wife, Carolyn, decided to start a winery on the property, they converted a pair of hop barns into the winemaking facility and tasting room, taking care to preserve the historic character of the buildings. Today, Lee Sr. and his two sons, Lee Jr. and George, do all the farming. References to the Martinelli farming heritage are visible in the homey tasting room store, where, amid rustic hutches stocked with linens and cottage-style dishware, ancient farm equipment and faded family photographs are on display.

MARTINELLI WINERY
3360 River Rd.
Windsor, CA 95492
800-346-1627
vinoinfo@
martinelliwinery.com
www.martinelliwinery.com

OWNERS: Lee Sr. and Carolyn Martinelli.

LOCATION: About 2 miles west of U.S. 101 via River Rd./Mark West Springs Rd. exit.

APPELLATION: Russian River Valley.

HOURS: 10 A.M.–5 P.M. daily.

TASTINGS: Complimentary.

TOURS: None.

THE WINES: Chardonnay, Muscat Alexandria, Pinot Noir, Sauvignon Blanc, Syrah, Zinfandel.

SPECIALTIES: Wines made from estate-grown grapes.

WINEMAKERS: Helen Turley, consulting winemaker; Bryan Kvamme, winemaker.

ANNUAL PRODUCTION: 12,000 cases.

OF SPECIAL NOTE: All wines are made from estate grapes. Gourmet foods available for purchase. Several picnic tables scattered throughout the property.

NEARBY ATTRACTIONS: Wells Fargo Center for the Performing Arts; Russian River (rafting, fishing, swimming, canoeing, kayaking).

MATANZAS CREEK WINERY

MATANZAS CREEK WINERY
6097 Bennett Valley Rd.
Santa Rosa, CA 95404
707-528-6464
800-590-6464
info@matanzascreek.com
www.matanzascreek.com

OWNERS: Jess Jackson and
Barbara Banke.

LOCATION: About 6 miles
southeast of Santa Rosa.

APPELLATIONS: Bennett
Valley, Sonoma Valley.

HOURS: 10 A.M.–4:30 P.M.
daily.

TASTINGS: $5 for 4 or
5 wines.

TOURS: By appointment,
10:30 A.M. and 2:30 P.M.
Monday–Friday and
10:30 A.M. Saturday.

THE WINES: Cabernet
Sauvignon, Chardonnay,
Merlot, Pinot, Rosé,
Sauvignon Blanc, Syrah.

SPECIALTIES: Chardonnay,
Merlot, Sauvignon Blanc.

WINEMAKER:
François Cordesse.

ANNUAL PRODUCTION:
40,000–45,000 cases.

OF SPECIAL NOTE: Extensive
garden. Picnic area beneath
oak trees with vineyard
views. Gift shop featuring
soap, sachets, grilling
sticks, and other items
made from estate-grown
lavender. Jackson Park
Merlot, Rosé, and Ultime
(red dessert wine) available
only at winery.

NEARBY ATTRACTIONS:
Luther Burbank Garden
and Home (tours of famed
horticulturist's property);
Charles M. Schulz Museum
(exhibits on *Peanuts* creator
and other cartoonists).

Matanzas Creek Winery presides over the picturesque Bennett Valley, one of the most serene and unspoiled of all California's winegrowing regions. Located between the Sonoma Valley and the city of Santa Rosa, the winery enjoys the best of both worlds: it is well off the beaten path yet easily accessed from several directions.

Founded in 1977 on the site of a former dairy farm, the original winery was replaced in 1985 with a modern winemaking demand for its Chardonnay addition to the complex is a ity, built in 2000. Over the past Winery's vineyard holdings have of Merlot and Syrah added in the estate plantings to more than 80 120-acre Jackson Park Vineyard

facility to accommodate growing and Merlot. The most recent barrel chai, a barrel-aging facil- three decades, Matanzas Creek doubled in size. New plantings late 1990s increased the total acres. The development of the (located across Bennett Valley

Road from the winery) in 1996 cemented Matanzas Creek Winery's leadership role in the Bennett Valley winegrowing community.

Surrounded by Taylor Mountain to the west, Sonoma Mountain to the south, and Bennett Peak to the east, the valley is cooled by coastal fog and breezes that drift northeast through the Crane Canyon gap and provide a long growing season that gives the grapes complex characteristics. The vines also benefit from a diversity of soil types, including deposits of ash on the valley floor from the surrounding volcanic peaks, as well as basalt, an ancient ocean-floor rock that imparts a slightly smoky character to the Matanzas Creek Merlot.

Matanzas Creek Winery began capitalizing on these attributes nearly three decades before Bennett Valley was recognized as an American Viticultural Area (AVA), one of the newest in Sonoma County. At one time defined as part of the county's Sonoma Valley and Sonoma Mountain AVAs, Bennett Valley overlaps with these regions but also carves out 8,150 acres to call its own. The appellation was formalized in 2003, although Bennett Valley's hospitable grape-growing environment was first discovered as early as the mid-1800s.

The winery was named after a nearby stream called Matanzas by the early Spanish for the Pomo Indian deer hunts that were once common in the area. It remains one of the few tasting rooms in the entire valley. Visitors are entranced with the winery's extravagant, terraced perennial gardens and its trademark one-acre plot of aromatic lavender. They can shop for souvenirs of the estate's lavender garden, including bath, beauty, home décor, and culinary products.

QUIVIRA VINEYARDS & WINERY

QUIVIRA VINEYARDS & WINERY
4900 West Dry Creek Rd.
Healdsburg, CA 95448
707-431-8333
quivira@quivirawine.com
www.quivirawine.com

OWNERS: Pete and Terri Kight.

LOCATION: About 4.5 miles northwest of Healdsburg via Dry Creek Rd. and Lambert Bridge Rd.

APPELLATION: Dry Creek Valley.

HOURS: 11 A.M.–5 P.M. daily.

TASTINGS: $5 for 5 tastes (applicable to wine purchase).

TOURS: Vineyard tours by appointment only ($15).

THE WINES: Grenache, Mourvèdre, Petite Sirah, Rosé, Sauvignon Blanc, Syrah, Zinfandel.

SPECIALTIES: Sauvignon Blanc, Zinfandel, Rhône varietals.

WINEMAKER: Steven Canter.

ANNUAL PRODUCTION: 13,000 cases.

OF SPECIAL NOTE: Picnic fare is available. Honey, preserves, and olive oil sold at winery. Twice a year, a 130-year-old fig tree produces fruit that can be sampled in the tasting room. Annual events include Winter Wineland (mid-January), Barrel Tasting weekends (early March), Passport Weekend (April), and Summer Solstice Lobster Boil (late June).

NEARBY ATTRACTIONS: Lake Sonoma (boating, camping, hiking).

This family-owned winery capped its steady journey toward becoming fully organic in 2005, when it was awarded organic and biodynamic certifications for its ninety-three acres of estate vineyards. Founded in 1981, the winery inaugurated its eco-practices in the late 1980s by starting a restoration project to enhance the steelhead and coho salmon population in Wine Creek, a seasonal waterway that bisects the property.

The 271-acre estate ranges from the banks of Dry Creek westward onto rolling benchlands. Proprietors Pete and Terri Kight, who bought Quivira in 2006, continue to produce the Sauvignon Blanc and Zinfandel that first attracted critical acclaim and are also growing Grenache and Petite Sirah, varieties widely planted in France's Rhône region, where the *terroir* is similar to Dry Creek's. Winemaker Steven Canter also oversees management of the vineyards with a proactive organic approach to agriculture, eschewing the use of chemicals and working as closely as possible with natural cycles.

At Quivira (pronounced "key-VEER-ah"), everything in the vineyards is produced organically on the property, from the soil on up. The winery makes olive oil from the fruit of its own trees as well as native wildflower honeys, courtesy of the bees that live on the estate. Friendly goats periodically roam the vineyards, eating weeds and unwanted grass, berries, and foliage. In the spring of 2008, work began on a one-acre organic garden, with pathways and seating to encourage visitors to linger among the fruit trees, vegetables, and flowers.

More outdoor seating is available around tables on the paved and pebbled patio in front of the tasting room. Housed in a steep-roofed, earth-toned hospitality center, the facility has natural cork flooring, a slate tasting bar, and a high, arched ceiling that, combined with wide paned windows, affords plenty of light and views across the vineyards toward Mount St. Helena. The building is topped with solar panels that generate all the energy for the winery.

A few yards behind the building, Wine Creek gurgles along, thanks to saplings planted to stabilize the banks and provide shade for the fish, which can rest among the rocks as they make their way upstream to spawn. The creek, which had suffered from the impact of human activities such as agriculture and mining that washed away or removed the gravel necessary for egg laying, has been successfully restored to the point that each spring the steelhead and coho can be spotted swimming and leaping in the shallow waters just as their ancestors did when the Pomo Indians lived here centuries ago.

RAMEY WINE CELLARS

RAMEY WINE CELLARS
25 Healdsburg Ave.
Healdsburg, CA 95448
707-433-0870
info@rameywine.com
www.rameywine.com

OWNERS: David and Carla Ramey.

LOCATION: .5 mile south of Healdsburg Plaza, via Central Healdsburg exit off U.S. 101.

APPELLATION: Russian River Valley.

HOURS: By appointment, Monday–Friday, 10 A.M. and 2 P.M.

TASTINGS: $25 for 6–8 current releases.

TOURS: None.

THE WINES: Cabernet Sauvignon, Chardonnay, Syrah.

SPECIALTIES: Single-vineyard Cabernet Sauvignon, Chardonnay, Syrah.

WINEMAKER: David Ramey.

ANNUAL PRODUCTION: 36,000 cases.

OF SPECIAL NOTE: Leisurely tastings last 1 hour.

NEARBY ATTRACTIONS: Riverfront Regional Park (hiking, fishing, boating, wildlife viewing); Russian River (swimming, canoeing, kayaking, rafting, fishing); Healdsburg Museum of History; Hand Fan Museum (collection of antique fans).

Some winemakers plan, plot, and scheme for years, if not decades, before they can establish their own winery. In David Ramey's case, the process was decidedly more casual, even spur-of-the-moment.

Not that he didn't have decades of experience before he founded Ramey Wine Cellars in 1996. Ramey had long been acknowledged as one of the pioneers who challenged the status quo among American winemakers and helped propel California into the spotlight on the international wine stage. From the start, Ramey has spent his entire career in the big leagues.

After a traditional beginning—a graduate degree from the University of California at Davis—Ramey struck out for France  for a stint at Château Pétrus in Pomerol, a small but distinctive wine region in Bordeaux known for producing opulent red wines. He returned to California the following year, French winemaking lessons learned, and was hired by Simi Winery in Healdsburg as assistant winemaker to Zelma Long. In 1984 he replaced the illustrious Merry Edwards as winemaker at Matanzas Creek and then spent six years at Chalk Hill Estate. During the 1990s, he also worked with Leslie Rudd, of Rudd Estate, and spent two years making Bordeaux-style wines at Dominus Estate (owned by Christian Moueix, of Pétrus).

It was at Dominus that Ramey had his "aha!" moment. Dominus made only red wines, but Ramey wanted to make whites as well. When Moueix told him he was welcome "to make a little Chardonnay on the side," Ramey seized the opportunity. Along with his wife, Carla, he produced his first wine under the Ramey Wine Cellars label, 260 cases of Chardonnay sourced from the prestigious Hyde Vineyard in the Carneros appellation.

It would be another five years before Ramey had a winemaking facility of his own. Still, it was hardly what could be called a grand plan: instead of creating a fancy estate, he set up shop in a warehouse located in a largely residential neighborhood in the heart of Healdsburg. In 2007, having outgrown the original space, Ramey opened a new winery a few blocks away in an industrial park. The warehouse is used mostly for red wines; the new facility, for whites.

The new site is unadorned, aside from the entrance, which is landscaped with soaring palms, delicate maple trees, and a smattering of native plants. Visitors are welcome to look around, but there are no tours, per se. Tastings are conducted in a second-floor room where sixteen people can be seated at a time, with nothing to distract them from focusing on the wines that Ramey handcrafts by fusing old-world traditions, California *terroir*, and New World innovations.

RAVENSWOOD WINERY

RAVENSWOOD WINERY
18701 Gehricke Rd.
Sonoma, CA 95476
707-938-1960
888-669-4679
www.ravenswood-wine.
com

OWNER: Constellation
Brands.

LOCATION: About .5 mile
northeast of the town of
Sonoma via Fourth St.
East and Lovall Valley Rd.

APPELLATION:
Sonoma Valley.

HOURS: 10 A.M.–4:30 P.M.
daily.

TASTINGS: $10 for county
series; $15 for vineyard-
designated wines.

TOURS: 10:30 A.M.
daily. Vineyard tour,
3 P.M., Monday–Friday,
seasonally.

THE WINES: Bordeaux-style
blends, Cabernet Franc,
Cabernet Sauvignon,
Chardonnay, Icon (blend
of Syrah, Mourvèdre, and
Grenache), Merlot, Petite
Sirah, Zinfandel.

SPECIALTY: Zinfandel.

WINEMAKER: Joel Peterson.

ANNUAL PRODUCTION:
500,000 cases.

OF SPECIAL NOTE: Blending
seminars by appointment.
Bicyclists and other
visitors are welcome to
picnic on stone patio with
view of vineyards.

NEARBY ATTRACTIONS:
Mission San Francisco
Solano and other historic
buildings in downtown
Sonoma; bike rentals; Vella
Cheese Company; Sonoma
Cheese Factory; Sonoma
Traintown (rides on a scale
railroad).

Few wineries set out to make cult wines, and probably fewer earn a widespread following as well. Ravenswood has done both. Its founders began by crushing enough juice to make 327 cases of Zinfandel in 1976, and although the winery also makes other wines, Zinfandel remains king. Nearly three-quarters of Ravenswood's production is Zinfandel.

Winemaker and cofounder Joel Peterson and chairman and cofounder Reed Foster were so successful with that first, handcrafted vintage that they have had to live up to the standard it set ever since. Ravenswood produces fourteen different Zinfandels that represent the spectrum of the varietal's per-sonality, with tastes ranging from peppery and spicy to chocolaty and minty. If there is one common denominator, it is reflected in the slogan adopted by the winery in 1990: "No Wimpy Wines."

Most of Ravenswood's grapes come from more than a hundred independent growers. It is those long-standing relationships that ensure the consistency of the wines. One vineyard source dates to 1986. The Strotz family invited Joel Peterson to visit their Sonoma Mountain vineyard, which they had named Pickberry because of all the wild blackberries harvested there. Peterson immediately recognized the quality of the Strotz grapes, and in 1988, Ravenswood released the first of its many blends of Cabernet Sauvignon, Cabernet Franc, and Merlot under the vineyard-designated name Pickberry.

Peterson never set out to specialize in Zinfandel; originally he was more interested in the Bordeaux varietals he began tasting at the age of ten with his father, Walter, founder of the San Francisco Wine Sampling Club. In time, however, he fell under the spell of Zinfandel. In the 1970s, after a brief career as a wine writer and consultant, he went to work for the late Joseph Swan, considered one of California's outstanding craftsmen of fine Zinfandel. Thus the stage was set for the varietal's ascendancy at the winery Peterson founded.

Ravenswood farms fourteen acres of estate vineyards on the northeast side of Sonoma. The old stone building, once home to the Haywood Winery, has extensive patio seating with beautiful south-facing views of the vineyards. Thanks to the company's growth, the winemaking operations have since been relocated to a forty-five-thousand-square-foot facility in the Carneros, to the south, but the tasting room remains. Originally a cozy, even cramped affair, it was greatly expanded in 1996, and now has plenty of elbow room as well as ample natural light for visitors who come to sample and appreciate the wines.

RAYMOND BURR VINEYARDS

RAYMOND BURR VINEYARDS
8339 West Dry Creek Rd.
Healdsburg, CA 95448
707-433-8559
RBurrwine@aol.com
www.raymondburr
vineyards.com

OWNER: Robert Benevides.

LOCATION: 8.5 miles
northwest of Healdsburg
via Dry Creek Rd. and
Yoakim Bridge Rd.

APPELLATION:
Dry Creek Valley.

HOURS: 11 A.M.–5 P.M. daily.

TASTINGS: Complimentary.

TOURS: None of winery.

THE WINES: Cabernet Franc,
Cabernet Sauvignon,
Chardonnay, Estate Port.

SPECIALTY: Hillside
Vineyard Cabernet
Sauvignon.

WINEMAKER:
Phyllis Zouzounis.

ANNUAL PRODUCTION:
3,000 cases.

OF SPECIAL NOTE:
Orchid greenhouse tours
on Saturdays and Sundays
by appointment; picnic
area with view of Dry
Creek Valley; monthly
food-and-wine tastings.

NEARBY ATTRACTIONS:
Lake Sonoma (boating,
camping, hiking, fishing,
swimming).

In 1986, some thirty years after the hit television show *Perry Mason* made Raymond Burr a household name, the actor decided to follow another passion: making great wine. The small Dry Creek Valley estate that bears his name does not produce enough grapes to find the worldwide audience of a hit TV series, but its reputation is growing.

Burr met fellow actor Robert Benevides on the set of *Perry Mason*, and they soon discovered that they shared an interest in appreciating wine and growing orchids. Eventually, the two friends turned both hobbies into viable commercial operations. In 1976 Benevides purchased forty prime acres of benchland at the foot of Bradford Mountain west of Healdsburg. As Burr's series *Ironside* was ending its eight-year run, the actor got his first look at the ranch. Burr must have been pleased: the view from the east-facing slopes of the property takes in a scenic swath of countryside, with hills and manzanita trees as far as the eye can see. In 1980 they relocated the commercial orchid nursery established several years earlier to their ranch and began developing the property.

The intimate, bungalow-style tasting room is filled with memorabilia from Raymond Burr's acting career, notably his Emmy awards and vintage issues of *TV Guide* with his picture on the covers. The space is cozy, so unless the weather is dismal, visitors take their glasses out to the patio, where they can be served in the shade of an old oak tree and take in the sweeping views. Sensational orchids can be seen in the greenhouses year-round, but fall is peak bloom season.

The fourteen-acre vineyard is on a steeply terraced hillside with very well-drained soil, ideal conditions for premium Cabernet Sauvignon grapes. Although the Dry Creek Valley is a warm growing region, the east-facing vineyards are bathed in shade late in the day, and the cool air from the nearby ocean keeps the temperatures low at night. The combination allows the grapes to mature at a steady pace. The longer the fruit hangs on the vine, the more flavor it develops. As Phyllis Zouzounis, who joined Raymond Burr Vineyards as winemaker in 2006, says, "Great wine is made in the vineyard with quality grapes." Currently the vineyard includes six acres of Cabernet Sauvignon, four acres of Chardonnay, and two acres of Cabernet Franc. Sadly, Burr's health deteriorated as the vineyards thrived, and he passed away in 1993. But a comment he made in a documentary about Northern California wines reflected his thinking about the vital, even intimate relationship between grape grower and land: "The most important things in a vineyard are the footprints of the grower between the rows."

SBRAGIA FAMILY VINEYARDS

Just before Dry Creek Road comes to its western terminus at Lake Sonoma, the Sbragia Family Vineyards winery, perched on a hill, comes into view. Visitors approach the winery on a winding driveway that passes through Zinfandel vineyards and lush gardens. Among the features they first see is the generous terrace overlooking the vineyards. The setting is an ideal one for an afternoon of tasting and enjoying the vista from the top of Dry Creek Valley, an impressive panorama that takes in Mount St. Helena on the eastern horizon.

Sbragia Family Vineyards is Ed Sbragia gained acclaim during winning wines at Beringer Vineyards in 2008. Seven years before he left wine under the Sbragia Family winery's name, the business is a duties with his son, Adam. Adam's many miles from the place where his thirty years of making award-in the Napa Valley before retiring Beringer, he had started producing Vineyards label. As reflected in the family affair. Ed Sbragia shares cellar wife, Kathy, is in charge of hospitality for the winery, and Ed's wife, Jane, and daughter, Gina, are often found behind the tasting bar.

The family's roots grow deepest in this part of Sonoma County. After purchasing land in Dry Creek Valley, the Sbragias grew and dried plums there for years. By the early 1960s, Ed's father, Gino Sbragia, had planted grapevines, which Ed helped tend until he went off to study chemistry at the University of California at Davis and then earn an enology degree at Fresno State. Gino Sbragia, who died in 1995, tried to start a winery, but Prohibition and the Great Depression prevented him from realizing his dream. Ed Sbragia promised his father that he would eventually establish a winery of his own. Among other endeavors, the family had run a bar called the Ark. That name is honored today at a private event space near the winery's tasting room.

Ed and Adam Sbragia's focus is on making vineyard-designated wines. Five, including Chardonnay, Sauvignon Blanc, Merlot, and two Zinfandels, are grown on estate vineyards ranging from five to thirteen acres. Another Zinfandel is sourced from a vineyard owned by Ed's uncle, and a friend's vineyard provides fruit for Cabernet Sauvignon. A Chardonnay and three Cabernet Sauvignons are from four of Ed Sbragia's favorite vineyards located in Napa Valley. A special Cabernet Sauvignon comes from one of the most sought-after vineyards in California, Sonoma Valley's Monte Rosso Vineyards. Of the estate vineyards, two are named in honor of Gino Sbragia. Gino's Vineyard was planted to Zinfandel more than two decades ago. La Promessa Vineyard, also producing Zinfandel, acknowledges Ed's fulfilled promise to his father.

SBRAGIA FAMILY VINEYARDS
9990 Dry Creek Rd.
Geyserville, CA 95441
707-473-2992
info@Sbragia.com
www.Sbragia.com

OWNERS: Ed Sbragia and Jane Sbragia.

LOCATION: 9 miles northwest of Healdsburg.

APPELLATION: Dry Creek Valley.

HOURS: 11 A.M.–5 P.M. daily.

TASTINGS: $5 for 3 or 4 wines for standard tasting; $10 for 3 or 4 wines for reserve tasting.

TOURS: By appointment only ($15 per person).

THE WINES: Cabernet Sauvignon, Chardonnay, Merlot, Sauvignon Blanc, Zinfandel.

SPECIALTIES: Cabernet Sauvignon, Chardonnay, Zinfandel.

WINEMAKERS: Ed Sbragia, Adam Sbragia.

ANNUAL PRODUCTION: 5,500 cases.

OF SPECIAL NOTE: Tables and chairs for picnicking on an expansive terrace with views; some prepared foods sold at winery. Annual events include Barrel Tastings (March), Passport Weekend (April), and Winter Wineland (January). Winery is pet friendly.

NEARBY ATTRACTIONS: Lake Sonoma (swimming, fishing, boating, camping, hiking).

SCHUG CARNEROS ESTATE WINERY

**SCHUG CARNEROS
ESTATE WINERY**
602 Bonneau Rd.
Sonoma, CA 95476
707-939-9363
800-966-9365
schug@schugwinery.com
www.schugwinery.com

OWNERS: Schug family.

LOCATION: .5 mile west of
intersection of Hwy. 121
and Hwy. 12.

APPELLATION: Los Carneros.

HOURS: 10 A.M.–5 P.M. daily.

TASTINGS: $5 (applicable
to wine purchase); $10 for
reserve tasting (applicable
to reserve wine purchase).

TOURS: By appointment.

THE WINES: Cabernet
Sauvignon, Chardonnay,
Merlot, Pinot Noir,
Sauvignon Blanc, Sparkling
Pinot Noir.

SPECIALTY: Pinot Noir.

WINEMAKER: Michael Cox.

ANNUAL PRODUCTION:
30,000 cases.

OF SPECIAL NOTE: Open
house in late April and in
mid-November (Holiday
in Carneros). *Pétanque*
court open to public.

NEARBY ATTRACTIONS:
Mission San Francisco
Solano and other historic
buildings in downtown
Sonoma; Infineon Raceway
(NASCAR and other
events); biplane flights;
Cornerstone Gardens
(innovative designs by
landscape architects).

Fog and wind from the Pacific Ocean and San Francisco Bay sweep along the low, rocky hills of the Carneros appellation, where the volcanic soil, laden with clay, is shallow and dense. Grape growers intent on producing Cabernet Sauvignon and many other premium varietals avoid these conditions at all costs. But Walter Schug wanted to grow Pinot Noir, and he knew that this challenging combination of climate and geology would bring out the best in his favorite grape.

Walter Schug first made his reputation in the 1970s as the acclaimed winemaker for Joseph Phelps. Working at the ultrapremium Napa Valley winery, he was successful with a range of wine grapes, notably Cabernet Sauvignon, before turning his attention to Pinot Noir. In 1980, beginning with grapes from a vineyard he had used at Phelps, Schug launched his own brand. Schug and his wife, Gertrud, selected a fifty-acre site in the southern Sonoma Valley for their new vineyard estate and crowned the hilltop with a winery in 1990. They favored post-and-beam architecture reminiscent of Germany's Rhine River Valley, where the Schug family had long produced Pinot Noir. The style makes it one of the most instantly recognizable wineries in the appellation. Pinot Noir and Chardonnay vineyards surround the winery, and Schug has long-term contracts with other growers in the Carneros to ensure the best grapes year after year. Protecting and enhancing the varietal and regional characteristics of the fruit are the essence of the Schug family's philosophy.

The European aspect of the Schug estate was enhanced with the excavation of an underground cave system in the mid-1990s. The system's naturally stable temperatures and humidity levels allow the wines to age gracefully in French oak barrels. Almost every inch of the caves is covered with gray concrete, but an exposed patch at the end of one tunnel affords a glimpse of the pockmarked, pumicelike volcanic rock characteristic of the region.

Visitors are warmly welcomed at this family-managed winery. From the hilltop tasting room, they are treated to spectacular views of the surrounding countryside. Nearby is a *pétanque* court, another nod to the Schugs' European ancestry. More than merely a sport, *pétanque* is a pastime that invites conviviality and conversation in the best old-world tradition.

SIDURI WINES

This is no-frills wine tasting at its best. Not only are there no sweeping driveways, grand architectural statements, or lavishly landscaped grounds, but there are virtually no signs directing drivers to Siduri. Hidden in a cul-de-sac in a neighborhood better known for chain stores and discount furniture outlets, the entrance is so low-key that first-time visitors might think they have to whisper a password to get in. Hardly, but they do need an appointment. Once inside the building, they won't have to wait in line or share the attention of the staff with a crowd of drop-ins.

Siduri's location in a warehouse may seem odd for a winery, but it fits the philosophy of its founders. Adam and Dianna Lee met in Dallas, where both were working for Neiman-Marcus—he as a wine buyer, she in the epicurean department. Native Texans and self-described wine geeks, they soon discovered their mutual love of Pinot Noir, especially those made in Sonoma by Tom Rochioli and Williams Selyem, two of the most notable Pinot producers of the last twenty-five years. They also shared a simple ambition: to move to California and "make killer Pinot Noir from the finest vineyards" they could find.

They established Siduri in 1994, naming it for the Babylonian goddess of wine who, according to myth and legend, held the wine of eternal life. With a conviction as big as the Texas sky, they figured they would learn winemaking as they went along. After they moved to California and got married, the Lees both worked at a number of small, family-owned wineries, which was a natural fit.

Believing that the best wines in the world come from low-yielding grapevines, Adam and Dianna Lee buy grapes by the acre rather than by the ton, so that growers can focus on low yields rather than high tonnage. The first Siduri release was 107 cases of 1994 Anderson Valley Pinot Noir Rose Vineyard. In the early days, the Lees made their wine at Lambert Bridge Winery in Dry Creek Valley, before establishing their own facility in 1998. Guided by the principle of concentrating on single-vineyard wines that reflect the personality of those sites, the Lees buy grapes from dozens of vineyards up and down the West Coast, from Oregon's Willamette Valley south to the Santa Rita Hills in Santa Barbara County.

There is something so intense about loving Pinot Noir that the varietal's most passionate fans are known as Pinot Noiristes. It is not surprising, then, that the vibe inside Siduri is akin to that of a secret club. At the appointed hour, visitors gather in front of a canyon of oak barrels in the "tasting room," where dozens of bottles are displayed atop upended wine barrels. The session also features wines from Novy Family Winery, which is owned by the Lees and Dianna's parents, brothers, and sisters-in-law.

SIDURI WINES
980 Airway Ct., Suite C
Santa Rosa, CA 95403
707-578-3882
pinot@siduri.com
www.siduri.com
www.novyfamilywines.com

OWNERS: Adam and Dianna Lee.

LOCATION: Off Airway Ct. between Industrial Dr. and Piner Rd., about .5 mile west of U.S. 101.

APPELLATIONS: Various in Oregon and California.

HOURS: By appointment, 10 A.M.–3 P.M. daily.

TASTINGS: Complimentary for 6–8 wines.

TOURS: Included with tasting.

THE WINES: Chardonnay, Grenache, Nebbiolo, Pinot Meunier, Pinot Noir, Syrah, Viognier, Zinfandel.

SPECIALTIES: Single-vineyard Pinot Noir and Syrah.

WINEMAKERS: Adam and Dianna Lee.

ANNUAL PRODUCTION: 12,000 cases.

OF SPECIAL NOTE: Annual events include Barrel Tasting (March) and Open Houses (summer and winter).

NEARBY ATTRACTIONS: Charles M. Schulz Museum (exhibits on *Peanuts* creator and other cartoonists); Sonoma County Museum (regional history and contemporary art and culture); Pacific Coast Air Museum; Luther Burbank Garden and Home (tours of famed horticulturist's property).

ST. FRANCIS WINERY & VINEYARDS

ST. FRANCIS WINERY & VINEYARDS
100 Pythian Rd.
Santa Rosa, CA 95409
888-675-WINE (9463)
info@stfranciswinery.com
www.stfranciswinery.com

PRESIDENT AND CEO:
Christopher Silva.

LOCATION: Off Hwy. 12,
6 miles east of Santa
Rosa and 1 mile west of
Kenwood.

APPELLATION: Sonoma
Valley.

HOURS: 10 A.M.–5 P.M. daily.

TASTINGS: $10 for 4 wines;
$30 for 3 wines paired with
food.

TOURS: Available for groups
of 10 or more with advance
reservations.

THE WINES: Cabernet Franc,
Cabernet Sauvignon,
Chardonnay, Mourvèdre,
Merlot, Petite Sirah, Port,
Rosé, Sauvignon Blanc,
Syrah, Zinfandel.

SPECIALTY: 100 percent
handpicked Sonoma
County grapes.

WINEMAKER: Tom Mackey.

ANNUAL PRODUCTION:
250,000 cases.

OF SPECIAL NOTE: Daily
extensive wine-and-food
pairings available from
11 A.M. to 4 P.M. ($30 or
$50). Monthly winery
dinners and educational
events listed online, with
information on summer
outdoor concert series.
Annual events include
Barrel Tasting (March).

NEARBY ATTRACTIONS:
Sugarloaf Ridge State
Park (hiking, camping,
horseback riding), Annadel
State Park (hiking, biking).

If St. Francis Winery & Vineyards wanted a catchy commercial come-on, it might be: Come for the wine, stay for the food. The winery was one of the first in California to offer an extensive wine-and-food pairing program and has never lost its leading edge. An executive chef is on staff to create innovative dishes to complement the winery's many food-friendly varietals.

The culinary focus began shortly after St. Francis relocated one mile north of its modest origins to a brand-new facility in 2001. Built  in the style of the early California missions, the red-tile-roofed, sand- colored stucco hospitality center is sited at the entrance of the vener- able Wild Oak Vineyard, with Hood Mountain as a backdrop. A tower near the tasting room features a bell that is rung to mark every hour. According to a plaque displayed on one side of the tower, the bell was cast by an historic Italian foundry and blessed in the Piazza della Basilica of St. Francis of Assisi.

Forty years ago, long before the wine world began to recognize the Sonoma County *terroir* as among the finest in the world, St. Francis Winery made the commitment to craft wines exclusively from Sonoma. The winery owns more than six hundred estate acres of prime vineyards in Sonoma Valley and Russian River Valley. Under the direction of winemaker Tom Mackey, each vineyard was planted row by row, block by block, with varietals particularly well suited to each site. St. Francis now reaps the rewards through a bounty of outstanding fruit from superior mountain and valley vineyards in Sonoma County's best appellations.

The first stop for most visitors is the tasting room, where the beamed ceiling soars over twenty feet, and warmth is provided by wood paneling—and, in winter, by a roaring fireplace. Tasting is available inside or out on the patio. There, umbrellas shade wooden tables and chairs arranged to create the best vista of the lawns, gardens, and Hood Mountain.

The Sonoma Valley's mild climate allows for being outdoors most of the year, especially from May through October. That time frame coincides with the winery's Wine and Charcuterie alfresco tasting. The rest of the year, wines and foods are paired indoors, particularly the Wine and Food Flight (November through April), which matches hors d'oeuvres with three wines. Throughout the year, wine-and-food pairings are available daily, with each session lasting forty or fifty minutes. Menus are changed seasonally to reflect the freshest products available locally. Typical is one served in the spring of 2008: shrimp and mango ceviche with Wild Oak Chardonnay; seared pork loin with Cabernet Franc; cremini mushroom stuffed with black truffle and parsley cream with a deep red wine; and a regional goat cheese matched with Cabernet Sauvignon.

STONESTREET

STONESTREET
7111 Hwy. 128
Healdsburg, CA 95448
800-355-8008
info@stonestreetwines.com
www.stonestreetwines.com

OWNER: Jess Jackson.

LOCATION: 6 miles north-northeast of Healdsburg, via Healdsburg Ave. and Alexander Valley Rd.

APPELLATION: Alexander Valley.

HOURS: 10 A.M.–5 P.M. daily.

TASTINGS: $7 for 3 wines; $18 for 3 reserve wines.

TOURS: None.

THE WINES: Cabernet Sauvignon, Chardonnay, Merlot.

SPECIALTIES: Estate and mountain vineyards.

WINEMAKER: Graham Weerts.

ANNUAL PRODUCTION: 18,000 cases.

OF SPECIAL NOTE: Most wines available only in tasting room and selected restaurants.

NEARBY ATTRACTIONS: Jimtown Store (country market, homemade foods).

Location may not be everything, but at Stonestreet, it speaks volumes. From the winery's Upper Barn Vineyard (elevation: 1,800 feet), the Mayacamas mountains, whose contours tell the story of the region's ancient volcanoes, are visible in clear detail. Rocks of all sizes, from boulders as large as buses to pea-sized gravel, tell the story of the mountaintops that exploded eons ago, raining volcanic minerals on the land below. Grapevines that are forced to struggle for survival amid these rocky soils tend to produce smaller berries and smaller yields per acre than those grown in loamy soil. Thus their fruit is more intense, a true reflection of the minerality of the vineyards.

The Upper Barn Vineyard is easily visible from the Stonestreet winery down on the valley floor. Visitors may enjoy tasting the wines all the more knowing how hard the vines had to work to produce every precious grape.

Jess Jackson, who made his first wine in 1982 under the Kendall-Jackson label, now one of the most popular brands in the country, established Stonestreet in 1989. In 1995 he purchased the Alexander Mountain Estate and merged the two properties to focus on fruit from the mountain vineyards, which range in elevation from 400 to 2,400 feet above sea level.

The Stonestreet winery was designed to fit in with the rural landscape and nearby vintage barns, and was painted to reflect the muted colors of the mountainsides. A tree-lined driveway extends nearly a mile from Highway 128 to the entrance, which is flanked by olive trees growing in terracotta urns. Directly across from the huge barn doors to the tasting room, a half-circle of healthy lawn arcs from the entrance in the direction of the winery's Alexander Mountain Estate; there and on the gravel terrace, several teak chairs and tables are arranged for leisurely gazing at the vineyards in the foreground and the mountains beyond.

The interior of the intimate tasting room, which opened in 2006, is done in muted tones of ivory and ocher. A grand alabaster chandelier floats above the bar, which is topped in smooth, polished concrete the color of ivory. French doors open onto the terrace, providing even more vistas of the Mayacamas. The only décor is a collection of moody mountain vignettes painted by Healdsburg designer Ann Shogren.

Stonestreet has gone to great lengths to preserve the natural setting of its 5,100 acres, fewer than 1,000 of which are planted to grapes. Eco-sensitive farming has allowed the uncultivated acreage to serve as a wildlife habitat for 150 species of fauna, including wild turkeys, coyotes, mountain lions, deer, foxes, peregrine falcons, and a variety of waterfowl.

ZICHICHI FAMILY WINERY

ZICHICHI FAMILY WINERY
8626 West Dry Creek Rd.
Healdsburg, CA 95448
707-433-4410
winery@zichichifamily
vineyard.com
www.zichichifamily
vineyard.com

OWNERS: Steve and Kristin
Zichichi.

LOCATION: About 7.5 miles
northwest of Healdsburg
via Dry Creek Rd. and
Yoakim Bridge Rd.

APPELLATION: Dry Creek
Valley.

HOURS: 11 A.M.–4:30 P.M.
daily.

TASTINGS: Complimentary.

TOURS: None.

THE WINES: Cabernet
Sauvignon, Petite Sirah,
Zinfandel.

SPECIALTIES: Estate-grown
Petite Sirah and old-vine
Zinfandel.

WINEMAKER:
Mikael Gulyash.

ANNUAL PRODUCTION:
4,000 cases.

OF SPECIAL NOTE: Barrel
tastings; picnic deck. Wines
are available only in the
tasting room and a handful
of local restaurants. Annual
events include Winter
Wineland (January) and
Passport Weekend (April).

NEARBY ATTRACTIONS:
Lake Sonoma (swimming,
fishing, boating, camping,
hiking).

As so often happens in stories about love at first sight, serendipity played a large role in the founding of this family winery. Steve and Kristin Zichichi made frequent visits to the California wine country from their home in New Orleans. In the mid-1990s, while vacationing in Sonoma Valley, the Zichichis decided on a whim to take a day trip out to Dry Creek Valley. That's when they were hit with the kind of lightning bolt that struck Michael Corleone in *The Godfather*. Totally smitten, they were beguiled by the area's similarities to Italy's Tuscan wine region and vowed to return.

Dedicated wine lovers, the Zichichis had long since set their hearts on eventually establishing their own winery. The couple wanted to raise their four children in the wine country but were solidly ensconced in New Orleans, where Steve Zichichi's career as a foot and ankle surgeon included working with the New Orleans Saints over the course of some nineteen years. In 2000, however, a Healdsburg real estate agent led them to an engaging property on West Dry Creek Road, a rambling byway that qualifies as one of the most scenic in Sonoma County. Entranced, the Zichichis decided to make a bid. Miraculously, although their bid was the lowest of six offers, they sealed the deal.

The former owners had been farming eighteen acres of vineyards and selling the grapes to St. Francis Winery in Sonoma Valley, a practice that Steve and Kristin Zichichi continued for several years while they began designing and building their own winery. When Hurricane Katrina devastated southern Louisiana in 2005, the family decided to make the move to Dry Creek Valley a bit ahead of schedule.

The Zichichi Family Winery has fourteen acres of old-vine Zinfandel and four of Petite Sirah vines, most of which were originally planted in the 1920s. The vines grow in rocky, gravelly soil on a gentle hillside that rolls down from the winery to Dry Creek itself. The view from the tasting room encompasses the vines and the rugged eastern hills beyond.

At the top of the knoll, the Zichichis built their winery to blend in with the surrounding countryside. The tasting room, opened in November 2006, sports a variety of woods: cedar for the ceiling, fir for the floor, a redwood back bar, and a counter topped with a plank of redwood. The natural materials include a fireplace hearth made of fieldstone.

In this inviting space, Steve Zichichi can be found six days a week, always eager to share his wines, sometimes straight from the barrel. Visitors can sip here or on the covered picnic deck, where they can also drink in the view.

MENDOCINO

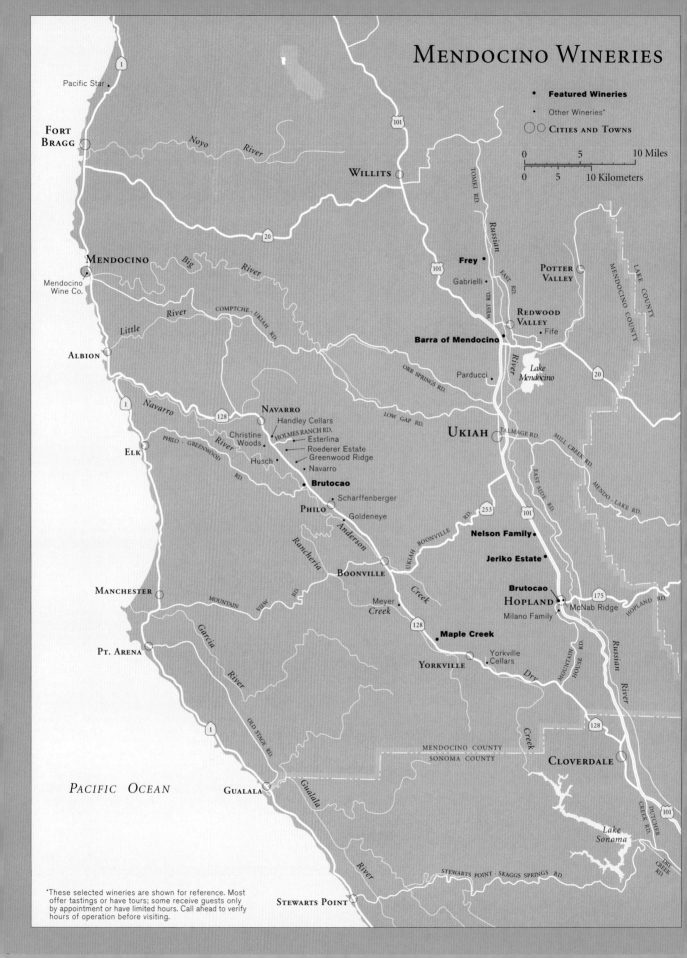

MENDOCINO WINERIES

● **Featured Wineries**

· Other Wineries*

○○ CITIES AND TOWNS

0   5   10 Miles

0   5   10 Kilometers

Pacific Star ·

FORT BRAGG

Noyo   River

WILLITS

101

Frey ·

Gabrielli ·

POTTER VALLEY

TOMKI RD.

Russian

EAST RD.

WEST RD.

20

REDWOOD VALLEY

Barra of Mendocino ·

· Fife

MENDOCINO COUNTY

LAKE COUNTY

MENDOCINO

Mendocino Wine Co. ·

Big   River

COMPTCHE - UKIAH RD.

River

Little

ALBION

ORR SPRINGS RD.

Parducci ·

Lake Mendocino

LOW GAP RD.

River

20

NAVARRO

Handley Cellars ·

HOLMES RANCH RD.

Christine Woods ·

· Esterlina

· Roederer Estate

· Greenwood Ridge

· Navarro

Husch ·

128

Navarro

River

PHILO - GREENWOOD RD.

1

Navarro

ELK

UKIAH

TALMAGE RD.

MILL CREEK RD.

MENDO - LAKE RD.

· **Brutocao**

· Scharffenberger

PHILO

· Goldeneye

Anderson

RD.

253

101

EAST SIDE RD.

UKIAH BOONVILLE

Nelson Family ·

Jeriko Estate ·

Rancheria

RD.

BOONVILLE

Creek

Meyer Creek ·

128

Brutocao

HOPLAND

Milano Family ·

· McNab Ridge

175

HOPLAND RD.

MOUNTAIN

VIEW

RD.

MANCHESTER

Maple Creek ·

Yorkville Cellars ·

YORKVILLE

MOUNTAIN HOUSE RD.

Russian River

Dry

PT. ARENA

Garcia

River

OLD STAGE RD.

1

Creek

128

MENDOCINO COUNTY

SONOMA COUNTY

CLOVERDALE

101

DUTCHER CREEK RD.

PACIFIC OCEAN

GUALALA

Gualala

River

Lake Sonoma

DRY CREEK RD.

River

STEWARTS POINT - SKAGGS SPRINGS RD.

STEWARTS POINT

*These selected wineries are shown for reference. Most offer tastings or have tours; some receive guests only by appointment or have limited hours. Call ahead to verify hours of operation before visiting.

Mendocino's dramatic coastline has made it famous all over the world, but the county offers a lot more than ocean views and rustic coastal inns. Now eyes are turning to inland Mendocino, where local winemakers are proving their grapes are on a par with those of nearby Sonoma and Napa.

Wine grapes were first planted here in the 1850s, when immigrants began farming food crops on the river  plains and vineyards on the rugged hillsides and sun-exposed ridgetops. In time, they and their successors found fertile ground in cooler areas that led them to achieve great success with a wide spec- trum of grape varietals.

Located too far north to transport their wines to the San Francisco market by boat—as Napa and Sonoma winemakers could—Mendocino's early grape growers sold and traded their crops closer to home. In the 1960s, the wine boom and advances in shipping brought Mendocino wines to markets farther afield. Today, the county boasts 72 bonded wineries, so many of them involving organic wines or vineyards that the county bills itself as "America's Greenest Wine Region."

Something of a pioneer spirit remains here and is reflected in a serious respect for the environment. Most of the county is an undeveloped, pristine landscape offering abundant opportunities for enjoying an endless variety of outdoor pursuits.

BARRA OF MENDOCINO

F ew, if any, people in the wine business can challenge Charlie Barra's record: he's been growing grapes since 1945. The wine world has changed dramatically since Charlie picked up
his first pair of pruning shears.

Barra was born eighty-one years ago to Italian immigrant parents who were accustomed to hard
work in the vineyards. They were attracted to the area because of its resemblance to Italy's Piedmont
region. As they farmed their new land, they were rewarded with a climate whose warm days and cool
nights allow the grapes to mature at a slow pace, thus producing intense flavors.

Like other Mendocino  grape growers, Barra came to
embrace a steward-of-the-land view of farming, a down-to-
earth attitude that propelled him toward sustainable agriculture. Aware that chemical pesti- cides were potentially endanger-
ing the vitality of his land, his workers, and the wildlife in the
vineyards, Barra stopped using them in 1985. Redwood Valley
Vineyards, the family's 175-acre home ranch, is certified annu-
ally by the California Certified Organic Farmers (CCOF).

Today, the Barra family produces three different wine brands using the grapes they grow organically at Redwood Valley Vineyards. The 1997 Petite Sirah was the first wine bottled under the
winery's premier brand, Barra of Mendocino. The Girasole Vineyards brand was born of the Pinot
Noir glut of 2001 that forced many growers to make a difficult choice: bottle the wine or sell it at
drastically reduced prices. The Barras decided to use their extra Pinot Noir to make a less expensive
wine, one with fresh, bright flavors and its own name, which means "sunflower" in Italian.

As a tribute to Charlie's sixty-plus years of farming, the family conceived the "59th Harvest."
Plans call for the label to change every year; the 2005 vintage will get its own label, "60th Harvest,"
and so on. The Barras are also introducing a vintage port under this label, starting with a 2005
Petite Sirah.

Barra of Mendocino opened its tasting room in 1995, located two miles down the road from
Redwood Valley Vineyards. The structure was built in 1972 by Weibel Champagne Cellars, which
may explain why it looks like an inverted shallow Champagne glass (minus the long stem). Beneath
the circular roof is a five-thousand-square-foot room with massive beams sweeping toward the
forty-foot-high ceiling and a fountain in the center. The tasting bar is set against the circular wall.
Outside, an expansive lawn and a carefully tended garden surround picnic tables that can seat up
to 180 people.

BARRA OF MENDOCINO
7051 North State St.
Redwood Valley, CA 95470
707-485-0322
info@barraof
mendocino.com
www.barraof
mendocino.com

OWNERS: Charles and
Martha Barra.

LOCATION: 8 miles north of
Ukiah via U.S. 101.

APPELLATION: Mendocino.

HOURS: 10 A.M.–5 P.M. daily.

TASTINGS: Complimentary.

TOURS: By appointment.

THE WINES: Cabernet
Sauvignon, Chardonnay,
Muscat Canelli, Petite
Sirah, Pinot Blanc, Pinot
Grigio, Pinot Noir, Port,
Sangiovese, Zinfandel.

SPECIALTIES: Petite Sirah,
Pinot Noir.

WINEMAKER: Dan Kopache.

ANNUAL PRODUCTION:
25,000 cases.

OF SPECIAL NOTE: Gardens
with picnic area. Gift shop
with wine accessories,
books, and apparel. Annual
events include A Taste of
Redwood Valley (June, on
Father's Day weekend);
Sunset at the Cellars (July);
and wild mushroom
gourmet dinners with
guest chefs (November).

NEARBY ATTRACTIONS:
Real Goods Solar Living
Center (tours, store);
Lake Mendocino (hiking,
boating, fishing, camping);
Grace Hudson Museum
(museum of art, history,
and anthropology); Vichy
Springs (mineral springs
and resort).

BRUTOCAO CELLARS

BRUTOCAO CELLARS
13500 U.S. 101
Hopland, CA 95449
800-433-3689
7000 U.S. 128
Philo, CA 95466
707-895-2152
brutocao@pacific.net
www.brutocaocellars.com

OWNER: Leonard Brutocao.

LOCATION: U.S. 101 in downtown Hopland; Hwy. 128 in Anderson Valley.

APPELLATION: Mendocino.

HOURS: 10 A.M.–5 P.M. daily.

TASTINGS: Complimentary.

TOURS: By appointment.

THE WINES: Cabernet Sauvignon, Chardonnay, Merlot, Pinot Noir, Port, Primitivo, Sauvignon Blanc, Syrah, Zinfandel.

SPECIALTIES: Cabernet Sauvignon, Merlot, Zinfandel.

WINEMAKER: Fred Nickel.

ANNUAL PRODUCTION: 12,000 cases.

OF SPECIAL NOTE: Crushed Grape Restaurant serving wood-fired pizza and California cuisine. Annual events include Valentine's Day Crabfeed (February), Hopland Passport (May and October), Anderson Valley Pinot Noir Festival (May), Big Bottles and Bocce BBQ (June), School Benefit Bocce Tourney (September), Port and Chocolate Tasting (November). Port and Syrah available only at tasting rooms.

NEARBY ATTRACTIONS: Real Goods Solar Living Center (tours, store); Hendy Woods State Park (hiking, camping).

Downtown Hopland was a quiet place with only a hotel, two modest restaurants, a brew pub, and the odd antique shop until the Brutocao family came to town. The Brutocaos, who had been making wine under their own label and already operated a tasting room in nearby Anderson Valley, decided to establish a presence on U.S. 101.

In 1997 Brutocao Cellars purchased the old Hopland High School from the Fetzer wine family and began creating a seven-and-a-half-acre complex dedicated to food and wine. Schoolhouse Plaza opened two years later with a tasting room and the Crushed Grape Restaurant in the remodeled 1920s building, which still has its original  facade bearing the high school's name. On display in the tasting room are memorabilia from the school's glory days. The complex also includes a large conference room, a full-service bar, and a tourist informa-tion area. Visitors can sip a glass of wine while perusing the large gift shop or can dine alfresco.

The Brutocaos, who trace their heritage to Italy, brought more than a love of food and wine when they came to this country. They are also passionate about bocce ball, a devil-ishly challenging game with a half-century Italian lineage. The complex has six regulation bocce (pronounced "BOTCH-ee") ball courts, which are lighted and open to the public.

With the remodeling complete, the winery set to work landscaping the grounds with some six thousand lavender plants and thirty-four hundred rosebushes. Between the terraces and the bocce ball courts is an expanse of manicured lawn with a peaked-roof gazebo that is used for outdoor weddings and other special events.

Brutocao Cellars is a tale of two families who combined their skills and expertise to establish one of Mendocino County's most notable wineries. The Brutocaos immigrated from Venice in the early 1900s, bringing with them a passion for wine. Len Brutocao met Marty Bliss while in school at Berkeley. Marty's father, Irv, had been farming land in Mendocino since the 1940s. Len and Marty married, and soon thereafter the families joined forces and began to grow grapes. The family sold their grapes to other wineries for years before starting to make their own wine in 1991. They selected the Lion of St. Mark from St. Mark's Cathedral in Venice as their symbol of family tradition and quality. The heart of that quality, they say, is in their 575 acres of vineyards in southern Mendocino County and another 12 acres (of Pinot Noir) in Anderson Valley. The original tasting room in Philo is still in use. With its high-beamed ceilings and wisteria-covered patio, it makes an ideal stop for those traveling scenic Highway 128 to the Pacific Coast.

FREY VINEYARDS, LTD.

FREY VINEYARDS, LTD.
14000 Tomki Rd.
Redwood Valley, CA 95470
707-485-5177
800-760-3739
info@freywine.com
www.freywine.com

OWNERS: Frey family.

LOCATION: 15 miles north
of Ukiah off U.S. 101.

APPELLATION:
Redwood Valley.

HOURS: By appointment.

TASTINGS: Complimentary.

TOURS: By appointment.

THE WINES: Cabernet
Sauvignon, Chardonnay,
Gewürztraminer, Merlot,
Petite Sirah, Pinot Noir,
Sangiovese, Sauvignon
Blanc, Syrah, Zinfandel.

SPECIALTIES: Certified
organic wines without
added sulfites; bio-
dynamically grown estate-
bottled wines.

WINEMAKERS: Paul Frey,
Jonathan Frey.

ANNUAL PRODUCTION:
100,000 cases.

OF SPECIAL NOTE: Picnic
area for visitors' use.

NEARBY ATTRACTIONS:
Real Goods Solar Living
Center (tours, store);
Lake Mendocino (hiking,
boating, fishing, camping);
Grace Hudson Museum
(Pomo Indian baskets,
historical photographs,
changing art exhibits);
Vichy Springs (mineral
springs and resort); Orr
Hot Springs (mineral
springs spa).

Arguably the most low-key winery in California, this gem is hidden off a two-lane road that wends through an undeveloped corner of Redwood Valley. Unsuspecting visitors might mistake the first building for the tasting room, but that's grandma's house. They must drive past it to reach the winery, and upon arriving, they find that there is no formal tasting room. Instead, tastings are conducted over a pair of wine barrels. When everyone retires to the original fashioned from an old barn—Visitors are encouraged to picnic and benches hand-hewn by the outdoors at a couple of planks set temperatures drop or rain falls, house—a redwood structure where the senior Mrs. Frey lives. at one of several redwood tables late family patriarch, Paul.

Virtually everything at this winery seems handmade or fashioned from something else. Barrels and tanks have been salvaged from larger operations, and the winery itself was constructed of redwood from a defunct winery in Ukiah. Some rows of grapevines are interplanted with herbs such as sage and oregano, which are harvested and distilled into aromatherapy products.

Frey (pronounced "fry") Vineyards is the oldest and largest all-organic winery in the United States. It may have another claim to fame as the winery with the most family members on the payroll. In 1961 Paul and Marguerite Frey, both doctors, bought ninety-nine acres near the headwaters of the Russian River. The Redwood Valley property seemed a great place to raise a family. Five of the couple's twelve children were born after the move, and most are still in the neighborhood.

In 1965 the Freys planted forty acres of Cabernet Sauvignon and Grey Riesling grapevines on the ranch's old pastureland, but they didn't start making wine until the 1970s. Eldest son Jonathan, who studied organic viticulture, began tending the vineyards and harvesting the grapes, which at first were sold to other wineries. When a Cabernet Sauvignon made with their grapes won a gold medal for a Santa Cruz winery, the family realized the vineyard's potential. Frey Vineyards was founded the next year, in 1980.

In 1996 the family began farming biodynamically. The word *biodynamic* stems from the agricultural theories of Austrian scientist and educator Rudolf Steiner. Biodynamic practices undertake to restore vitality to the soil. The farm is managed as a self-sustaining ecosystem, using special composting methods and specific planting times. As good stewards of the land, Frey started the first organic winery and was the first American winery fully certified by Demeter, the biodynamic certification organization. The wines have won many gold and silver medals for excellence.

JERIKO ESTATE

JERIKO ESTATE
12141 Hewlitt and
Sturtevant Rd.
Hopland, CA 95449
707-744-1140
info@jerikoestate.com
www.jerikoestate.com

OWNER: Daniel Fetzer.

LOCATION: About 2 miles
north of Hopland via
U.S. 101.

APPELLATION: Mendocino.

HOURS: 10 A.M.–5 P.M.
daily.

TASTINGS: $5 for 7 wines.

TOURS: By appointment.

THE WINES: Chardonnay,
Grenache Noir, Merlot,
Pinot Noir, Sangiovese,
Sauvignon Blanc, Syrah.

SPECIALTIES: *Méthode
champenoise* Brut and
Brut Rosé.

WINEMAKER: George Vierra.

ANNUAL PRODUCTION:
25,000 cases.

OF SPECIAL NOTE: Several
picnic sites around the
estate; gourmet food
products available in
tasting room. Annual
events include Hopland
Passport Weekend (May
and October). Brut Rosé,
Grenache Noir, and
Sauvignon Blanc available
only in tasting room.

NEARBY ATTRACTIONS:
Grace Hudson House
(museum of art, history,
and anthropology); Held-
Poage Memorial Home
and Research Library
(Mendocino County
history); Real Goods
Solar Living Center
(tours, store).

The Fetzer family has been a major force in Mendocino County winemaking for decades, ever since Barney and Kathleen Fetzer produced their first commercial wine vintage in 1968 from grapes grown on an estate they had bought ten years earlier. The family is also acclaimed for having pioneered organic grape growing in California.

Skip forward to 1997, when Daniel Fetzer, Barney and Kathleen's son, began planting Pinot Noir, Chardonnay, Syrah, Merlot, Sauvignon Blanc, and Sangiovese grapes on his own 200-acre ranch just north of Hopland. Now, he farms 120 acres of estate vineyards that extend from the foothills eastward, all the way across U.S. 101 to the Russian River. Staying true to his family heritage in another way, Fetzer uses organic farming techniques. He released his first vintage, a Chardonnay, in 2000, but his most precious claim to fame is the distinction of having produced the county's first organic sparkling wine, a Brut, in 2001.

Fetzer decided to name his winery Jeriko Estate, evoking the ancient city of Jeriko in the region where plants and animals were first domesticated. Visitors approach the winery through a series of formidable iron gates that Fetzer embellished with crests and flanked with imposing stone columns of his own design. The view from the road offers a panoramic display of early California and Mediterranean-style architecture expressed in dun-colored, low-rise buildings topped with red tile roofs. Irregularly spaced, statuesque Canary Island date palms punctuate the Mediterranean influence. Olive trees have been planted around the visitor center. In front of the entrance, low stone walls surround a manicured field of grass divided into quadrangles in the formal Italian style. Sheep and goats can often be seen grazing around the vineyards closest to the winery, and ducks and other wildlife frequent the estate's ponds.

Behind the winemaking facility stands the original estate residence, built in 1898 by San Francisco Judge J. H. Sturtevant. Daniel Fetzer extensively redesigned the structure a century later for use as a hospitality center for VIPs. The home's color scheme provided the inspiration for the adjacent winery and visitor center, constructed in 1999. Inside the center, soaring glass walls enclose the enormous barrel room where stack after stack of aging wine is easily visible from every angle. Also on display is a casual exhibit of historic winemaking equipment, including an antique French riddling rack once used in the production of *méthode champenoise* sparkling wines.

In a corner near the tasting bar, a pair of comfortably worn leather sofas are arranged in a conversational grouping in front of a giant fireplace whose hearth extends all the way to the high ceiling.

MAPLE CREEK WINERY

In late winter and early spring, drivers along scenic Highway 128 west can see young lambs cavorting in the fields, buckeye trees blooming on the hillsides, and vineyard rows bursting in crimson clover and yellow mustard. Throughout the year, apple and pear orchards, small farms, and winding roads make this part of Mendocino one of the most beautiful drives in California. The area is characterized by family-owned wineries where the owners and winemakers are often available to greet you. Maple Creek Winery is one of the little treasures that you'll find in this relaxed, country setting.

That potential for an intimate experience was one of the factors in Linda Stutz's and Tom Rodrigues's decision to open their own winery. Linda was a commercial interior designer working in Marin and San Francisco. Tom had established himself as a successful artist in media ranging from stained glass to wine labels, such as those for Far Niente, Dolce, and Nickel & Nickel in Napa Valley, and was also known for his fine art oil painting. Both wanted to pursue their dream of living in the country with horses, cats, and dogs, growing a big organic garden, having a fruit orchard, and living off the land. Mostly, they wanted to grow grapes, make wine, and enjoy the fruits of their labor.

In 2001 Stutz and Rodrigues made the leap of faith and purchased a 181-acre ranch in Yorkville, far from the hectic urban environment of the San Francisco Bay Area. The property includes seven natural springs, pastureland, and forests, and supports an array of wildlife. Bordering the property is Maple Creek, the winery's namesake. Today, they farm 10 acres of sustainable vineyards that produce fruit for the winery's award-winning Merlot and Chardonnay. They also purchase grapes from local growers who use either sustainable or organic farming methods.

Stutz and Rodrigues set to work transforming an old farm building into their rustic tasting room. They decorated it with numerous paintings and other works by Rodrigues, ranging from a portrait of baseball player Cool Papa Bell (the original hangs in the Hall of Fame in Cooperstown, New York) to pastoral scenes of Anderson Valley, which adorn the winery's Artevino label. The name was chosen for the label to represent their twin interests. Rodrigues is also Maple Creek's winemaker and pursues this passion with guidance from consulting winemaker Kerry Damskey.

Tom Rodrigues and Linda Stutz recognize that farming and winemaking go hand in hand. The Yorkville Highlands appellation in southern Mendocino offers an inspiring backdrop for their many creations.

MAPLE CREEK WINERY
20799 Hwy. 128
Yorkville, CA 95494
707-895-3001
wine@maplecreekwine.
com
www.maplecreekwine.com

OWNERS: Tom Rodrigues and Linda Stutz.

LOCATION: 19 miles northwest of Cloverdale.

APPELLATION: Yorkville Highlands.

HOURS: 10:30 A.M.–5 P.M. daily.

TASTINGS: $5 (applicable to purchase).

TOURS: None, except at harvest, when you can see the crush and winemaking.

THE WINES: Chardonnay, Merlot, Pinot Noir, Symphony, Zinfandel.

SPECIALTIES: Chardonnay, late-harvest wines, Bordeaux-style wines.

WINEMAKER: Tom Rodrigues.

ANNUAL PRODUCTION: 3,500 cases.

OF SPECIAL NOTE: Tasting room/art gallery features work of owner Tom Rodrigues. Picnic setting available. Most of the wines are sold only at the tasting room. Local events include Crab & Wine Days (January), Yorkville Highlands Wine Festival (August), and Mendocino Wine Affair (September).

NEARBY ATTRACTIONS: Hendy Woods State Park (redwood groves, hiking, camping).

157

NELSON FAMILY VINEYARDS

NELSON FAMILY VINEYARDS
550 Nelson Ranch Rd.
Ukiah, CA 95482
707-462-3755
tastingroom@
nelsonvineyards.com
www.nelsonfamily
vineyards.com

OWNER: Nelson and Sons Inc.

LOCATION: About 6 miles north of Hopland via U.S. 101.

APPELLATION: Mendocino.

HOURS: 10 A.M.–5 P.M. daily.

TOURS: By appointment.

TASTINGS: Complimentary for all wines.

THE WINES: Cabernet Sauvignon, Chardonnay, Orange Muscat, Pinot Grigio, Pinot Noir, Riesling, Viognier, Zinfandel.

SPECIALTIES: All wines are estate grown. "Top Row" Reserve Cabernet Sauvignon is sourced from a single row at top of Clara's Terrace.

WINEMAKER: Christopher Nelson.

ANNUAL PRODUCTION: 1,300 cases.

OF SPECIAL NOTE: Winemaker is often pouring wine in the tasting room. Winery is kid and pet friendly. Fresh strawberries available May–October at stand near winery entrance. Annual events include Hopland Passport Weekend (May and October).

NEARBY ATTRACTIONS: Grace Hudson House (museum of art, history, and anthropology).

The northern end of Sanel Valley doesn't seem to have changed all that much since 1952, when Herman and Clara Nelson sold their apricot farm in the San Jose area and moved up to Mendocino County. They settled on a two-thousand-acre spread between Hopland and Ukiah, where, at the time, wineries were few and far between along this stretch of U.S. 101. The Nelsons established a farm that has evolved over the decades from growing plums and raising sheep to growing Bartlett pears, Christmas trees, and, most importantly, grapes.

The Nelsons might recognize the old farmstead today, especially since most of the ranch remains undeveloped rangeland, consistent with the Sanel Valley landscape. Only from a distance, though, would they spot the little house they used to live in. That has been transformed into a chic tasting room with an ultra-modern color scheme of lime

green and lilac. A sleek white fireplace occupies a corner across the small room from an uncluttered counter fashioned from madrone and black walnut trees that grew on the property until they were cut down in 1987 to make room for the private road.

On the front porch, a pair of slatted redwood tables topped with market umbrellas face the garden, where a gravel path meanders beside fruit trees interspersed with Mediterranean-climate plants like lavender and native grasses. Typical of a county where everyone seems to know everyone else, the landscaping was done by the much-lauded Kate Frey, who designed the acclaimed organic gardens at Fetzer's Valley Oaks in nearby Hopland.

A lot more than the house and gardens has changed since grandson Chris Nelson, who had been living in the San Francisco Bay Area, returned to his childhood home to take up the family farming tradition. Nelson, who has a degree in mechanical engineering, had worked at Summerwood Winery in Paso Robles before deciding to establish his own winery.

The winery is a true family operation. Chris works alongside his brother, Tyler, and his father, Gregory, who manage the vineyards. With more than sixty years of vineyard experience, they have chosen the ideal locations for each varietal, such as the terraced, quick-draining slope where Cabernet Sauvignon does best and the low-lying gravelly soil that naturally slows the fast-growing tendencies of Zinfandel vines. In all, they now tend more than two hundred acres planted with nine varietals, including Zinfandel, Carignane, Pinot Grigio, Cabernet Sauvignon, Viognier, Orange Muscat, Riesling, Pinot Noir, and Merlot. In this quiet rural setting, visitors can enjoy the wines and the ambience of a timeless valley.

ACKNOWLEDGMENTS

Creativity, perseverance, and commitment are important qualities for guaranteeing the success of a project. The artistic and editorial teams who worked on this edition possess these qualities in large measures. My heartfelt thanks go to Marty Olmstead, writer; Robert Holmes, photographer; Judith Dunham, copy editor; Linda Bouchard, proofreader; The Book Designers, production; and Ben Pease, cartographer.

In addition, I am grateful for the invaluable counsel of Chester and Frances Arnold; Greg Taylor; William Silberkleit; Estelle Silberkleit; my late-night crisis administrator, Danny Biederman; and the scores of readers and winery enthusiasts who have contacted me to say how much they enjoy this book series.

And finally, for her love, support, and creative input, as well as for enduring work-filled weekends and midnight deadlines, my gratitude and affection go to Lisa Silberkleit.

—Tom Silberkleit

Photographs copyright © 2009 by Robert Holmes
Text and maps copyright © 2009 by Wine House Press
All rights reserved. No text, photographs, maps, or other portions of this book may be reproduced in any form without the written permission of the publisher.

Wine House Press
127 East Napa Street, Suite F, Sonoma, CA 95476
707-996-1741

Editor and publisher: Tom Silberkleit
Original design: Jennifer Barry Design, Fairfax, CA
Production: theBookDesigners
Copy editor: Judith Dunham
Cartographer: Ben Pease
Artistic development: Lisa Silberkleit
Proofreader: Linda Bouchard

All photographs by Robert Holmes, except the following: page 20, bottom left: Andy Berry Photography; page 32: Margot Hartford Photography; page 36, bottom left, and page 37: John Bedell Photography; page 94, bottom left, and page 95, courtesy Ferrari-Carano Vineyards & Winery; page 105, bottom right: Lenny Siegel Photographic; pages 112 and 113: M. J. Wickham; page 117, bottom left: Forrest Galt Photography; page 125, bottom left: Mary Fish; page 128: Peter Griffith.

Front cover photograph: Vineyards in Los Carneros, Napa
Back cover photographs: top left: Domaine Carneros; top right: Robert Mondavi Winery; bottom left: Swanson Vineyards; bottom right: Mumm Napa.

Printed and bound
in Singapore through DNP America, LLC

ISBN-13: 978-09724993-4-7

Fourth Edition

Distributed by Ten Speed Press, P.O. Box 7123, Berkeley, CA 94707, www.tenspeed.com

The publisher has made every effort to ensure the accuracy of the information contained in *The California Directory of Fine Wineries,* but can accept no liability for any loss, injury, or inconvenience sustained by any visitor as a result of any information or recommendation contained in this guide. Travelers should always call ahead to confirm hours of operation, fees, and other highly variable information.

Always act responsibly when drinking alcoholic beverages by selecting a designated driver or prearranged transportation.

Customized Editions
Wine House Press will print custom editions of this volume for bulk purchase at your request. Personalized covers and foil-stamped corporate logo imprints can be created in large quantities for special promotions or events, or as premiums. For more information, contact Custom Imprints, Wine House Press, 127 E. Napa Street, Suite F, Sonoma, CA 95476; 707-996-1741.

OTHER BOOKS BY WINE HOUSE PRESS

The California Directory of Fine Wineries—Central Coast
Santa Barbara • San Luis Obispo • Paso Robles